Seeing What Qohelet Saw

Seeing What Qohelet Saw

The Structure of Ecclesiastes as Alternating Panels of Observation and Wisdom

Douglas R. Fyfe

WIPF & STOCK · Eugene, Oregon

SEEING WHAT QOHELET SAW
The Structure of Ecclesiastes as Alternating Panels of Observation and Wisdom

Copyright © 2019 Douglas R. Fyfe. All rights reserved. Except for brief quotations in critical publications or reviews, no part of this book may be reproduced in any manner without prior written permission from the publisher. Write: Permissions, Wipf and Stock Publishers, 199 W. 8th Ave., Suite 3, Eugene, OR 97401.

Wipf & Stock
An Imprint of Wipf and Stock Publishers
199 W. 8th Ave., Suite 3
Eugene, OR 97401

www.wipfandstock.com

PAPERBACK ISBN: 978-1-7252-5297-4
HARDCOVER ISBN: 978-1-7252-5298-1
EBOOK ISBN: 978-1-7252-5299-8

Manufactured in the U.S.A.   DECEMBER 6, 2019

Unless otherwise noted, all translations of Hebrew and German are the author's own.

For Callum:

וזכר את־בוראיך בימי בחורתיך
עד אשר לא־יבאו ימי הרעה
והגיעו שנים אשר תאמר אין־לי בהם חפץ:

Ecclesiastes 12:1

CONTENTS

Preface | ix
Acknowledgments | xi

PART 1: The History of the Search for a Structure | 1
    Background | 1
    Historical Approaches | 2
    Why ראה? | 21
    Summary | 28

PART 2: The Observation Panels | 30
    Observation Panels in Summary | 30
    Observation Panels in Detail | 32
    Conclusion | 72

PART 3: The Wisdom Collections | 73
    The View of the Epilogue Regarding the Rest of the Book | 73
    Qohelet among the Sages | 75
    The Four Wisdom Panels in Detail | 78
    Summary of the Relationship between Observation and Wisdom Panels | 93
    The Two Interludes | 94
    Summary | 97

PART 4: The Book's Bookends | 99
    The Internal Bookends | 100
    The External Bookends | 105
    The Two Pairs of Bookends Together | 109

CONCLUSION | 115

Bibliography | 117

PREFACE

While the suggestions on a structure of Ecclesiastes are myriad, where this solution differs is that it both follows the contours of others as well as forging new ground. Combining the suggestions of paneling or alternation with the search for keywords, the proposal in this book is that the structure of Ecclesiastes is one of alternating panels of first-person observation and collected wisdom, with the keyword of ראה (to see) giving structure to the observation panels.

This book begins with a historical review of the attempts to find a structure of the centuries and the converging of those attempts into the current one. The second part investigates the use of ראה to give structure to the observation panels as a whole, but also the individual units of each panel. The third part looks at the wisdom collections, which alternate with the observation panels, and considers their relationship to the narration with which they alternate. The fourth and final part investigates the bookends and shows how they foreshadow and conclude the type of structure of the body of the book which is proposed in this structure.

The goals of this book are to present a convincing structure of Ecclesiastes, which will enable people to read the book according to the alternating genres of observation and wisdom, and also to provide a common footing and even a common structural language for examining the other questions which dominate Ecclesiastes research today.

ACKNOWLEDGMENTS

Many thanks to George Athas for his sage advice and continued encouragements to argue better. Thanks also for Paul Williamson for supervising in George's absences, especially for suggestions on the structure of my argument and his very quick turnaround in reading. My work is much improved from their advice, and any errors or flaws in arguments are my own.

It would also be remiss of me not to thank Northern District Chinese Christian Church Sydney for their support of my studies and for allowing time to focus on this work. This also means thanks to the congregations of ND for letting me muddle through numerous sermons on Ecclesiastes, as well as those other churches who have invited me to preach at services and weekends away, as I have tested out this structure in the wild.

The forbearance and encouragement of my family have kept me going through the roller coaster that is writing a research thesis.

PART 1:
The History of the Search for a Structure

Background

Ecclesiastes is a really difficult book. The goal of this book—discerning the structure Ecclesiastes—is just one of a number of questions which have found little widespread agreement. Other similarly contentious issues include the questions of dating and authorship, the *Redaktionsgeschichte* (how the book came together), as well as the tone in which we are supposed to read the book. These are indeed important issues, and my hope is that the structure of Ecclesiastes presented in this book will help those trying to think through various questions relating to Ecclesiastes to at the very least have a common starting point for reading the book according to the divisions revealed by this structure.

At the outset I should be very clear that the structure presented in this book is not exclusive to any understanding of the tone, dating, and authorship of Ecclesiastes. My own views on these things will come through in the book, but views different than my own do not affect the way the structure I have presented here is to be understood.[1] Nevertheless, it is worth briefly mentioning my approach to the *Redaktionsgeschichte*. I side with those

---

1. For the record, on dating I follow the consensus with a postexilic dating, and on tone I am more inclined towards Luther's optimism rather to than Jerome's pessimism.

who perceive one hand behind the final product. That is, it makes most sense to me that Qohelet (the main character of Ecclesiastes, whose words appear in the body of the book) is the literary creation of the author, and it is he whose journey and findings we follow, while his words are framed by a frame narrator. As Fox, who best explicated the idea of the frame narrator, explains, "I suggest that all of 1:2—12:14 is by the same hand—not that the epilogue is by Qohelet, but that *Qohelet* is 'by' the epilogist."[2] Therefore, when talking about the body of the book, it is appropriate to speak of the words of Qohelet as well as the words of the author. However, when speaking of the introduction and conclusion to Qohelet's words, it is appropriate to speak of the author or frame narrator. From a practical point of view, this frees readers up to work from the final form of the book, sitting as "listeners" without the need to go behind the text to determine (or speculate about) redactional layers. That is, whatever the history may have been, the final form of the text is what we must deal with, rather than any hypothetical *Urtext* or rearranged reconstruction.

What this book will do then is outline in detail a structure which, from a structural point of view, responds to cues in the text and brings together and develops previous approaches in elucidating a structure. From an heuristic perspective this structure will aid reading and allow the reader to get into the mindset of the author.

Historical Approaches

There have been various approaches to discerning the structure of the book, and there are plenty of good summaries elsewhere. Wright, for instance, worked chronologically through his predecessors, describing two types of approaches before him, with himself as a new third way. The first group he described saw no structure at all, while the second discerned "some unity or progression of thought." He styled himself the leader of a third group,

---

2. Fox, "Frame-Narrative and Composition," 91. Italics original.

PART 1: THE HISTORY OF THE SEARCH FOR A STRUCTURE

the beginnings of the "New Stylistics" or the "New Critics."[3] Fifty years on from Wright, Holmstedt, Cook and Marshall note a similar threefold division: a first group who found no structure as they understood the book to be a collection of aphorisms, a second who saw a progression tied to key phrases, while a third thought "Qohelet's ramblings reflect[ed] his disturbed psychological state."[4] Holmstedt et al. are perhaps a little reductionistic in their diagnosis of the state of play, while Wright precedes (but also probably prompted!) much of the more recent work on the structure, which will be discussed below. From my perspective, the approaches can be grouped into the following five approaches:

1. No structure at all, which means a disordered book, and any suggestions of structure are only false leads;
2. Collected aphorisms, akin to the book of Proverbs; this may mean some logic to some of the groupings, but by and large any structure must be provided externally to the book;
3. Logical progression, such as telling a story, or a memoir;
4. Keywords are placed deliberately in the text as indicators of structure;
5. Paneling (or alternation) between different genres or emphases within the book.

Generally speaking, all interpreters' approaches can be situated within at least one of these groupings and sometimes into more than one.

1. No Structure

That the book has no structure, or at least no discernible structure, was the rather resigned conclusion of several authors in the eighteenth and nineteenth centuries. **Bishop Lowth**, writing in the middle of the eighteenth century, summed up the state of play at

---

3. Wright, "Riddle of the Sphinx," 314–18.
4. Holmstedt et al., *Qoheleth*, 2.

that time, writing, "Scarcely any two commentators have agreed concerning the plan of the work, and the accurate division of it into parts or sections."[5] Things had not improved a century later, with the famous comments by **Franz Delitzsch** declaring the matter as good as closed: "All attempts to show, in the whole, not only oneness of spirit, but also a genetic progress, an all-embracing plan, and an organic connection, have hitherto failed, and must fail."[6]

Over time more scholarly endeavor was given to the task, with various structures being suggested, but several more recent authors have suggested there is indeed no structure, at least on the larger scale. The first of these is **J. A. Loader**, whose focus is on seeming contradictions in Ecclesiastes. However, rather than seeing confusion, he sees tensions raised through the "polar structures" in Qohelet's words. Qohelet is for Loader someone grasping for meaning, and somewhere in the tensions created by the polar opposite positions he expresses, meaning is to be found.[7]

For completely different reasons, **Jacques Ellul** deliberately resists imposing a grand structure on the book, claiming that this Western impulse is both "anachronistic" and "distinctly Cartesian."[8] This is not to say material is not able to be grouped; Ellul identifies thirty-two sections which can all be summarized as Qohelet's meditations on either vanity, wisdom or God. These three "maxims" drive Qohelet's deliberations and enable the reader to trace the threads of his thought.

More recently **Tremper Longman III**[9] and **Craig Bartholomew** have also refrained from making firm statements on structure. They divide the text into smaller sections, attempting to identify seams between Qohelet's thoughts, with Bartholomew in

---

5. Lowth, *Lectures*, 342.
6. Delitzsch, *Commentary*, 188.
7. Loader, *Polar Structures*.
8. Ellul, *Reason for Being*, 34.
9. "I do not find a clear and obvious structure." Although compare with his statement one page earlier that "the general structure of the book is clear." Longman, *Book of Ecclesiastes*, 23.

PART 1: THE HISTORY OF THE SEARCH FOR A STRUCTURE

particular building on Loader's work on tension and Ellul's idea of Qohelet drifting from subject to subject.[10]

Similarly, **Michael V. Fox** sees similarities between the style of Ecclesiastes and Wittgenstein's self-description, as they both pursue their "philosophical investigations [...], report[ing] a journey of a consciousness over the landscape of experience [...], a landscape generally lacking highways and signposts, order and progression."[11]

These commentators have concluded that there is no larger structure to the book of Ecclesiastes. They are latching on to the observations that Qohelet does seem to jump around, that his thoughts seem to be in tension with one another, and that a grand structure does not immediately jump out at the reader.

Trying to understand why someone would write a work with no structure has indeed puzzled many, such that one farcical (yet anachronistic) suggestion—which would solve the apparent lack of order—involves the loose-leaf pages of what was previously a well-ordered text being dropped, becoming muddled as it was incorrectly reassembled, and no one since has been able to restore it to its previous order.[12]

Funnily enough, this is not hugely different to **Martin Luther**'s position, which was that Ecclesiastes is disordered, and has been mashed together in a way not dissimilar to his own *Tischreden*.[13] He does note some points at which movements in the text might be noted, but concludes that any apparent structure has no impact on the message; for him the only structure he was aware of has as much impact on the reader as a sock-clad Luther quietly padding around the monastery.[14] If Qohelet had more clearly

10. Bartholomew, *Ecclesiastes*, 82–83.
11. Fox, *Qohelet and His Contradictions*, 158.
12. Bickell, *Prediger über den Wert des Daseins*, 1–45.
13. "Daher auch keyne ordenung ynn disen büchern gehallten ist, Sondern eyns yns ander gemengt, wie sie es nicht alles zu eyner zeyt, noch auff eyn mal von yhm gehört haben, wie solcher bücher art seyn mus." WADB 10.2.104, as cited in Wolters, "Ecclesiastes and the Reformers," 63.
14. "Dies Buch sollt völliger seyn, ihm ist zu viel abgebrochen, es hat weder Stiefel noch Sporn, es reitet nur in Socken, gleichwie ich, da ich noch

5

ordered his book, or so the logic follows, then its purpose would be clearer, and more people would be more greatly impacted by this book. Instead the readers are left with a book with no structure because whoever compiled the book took no care to order it better.

Of course this does not solve the question of structure. It simply "kicks it down the road" for the source critics to pick up. The beginnings of such an approach can be found with **C. Siegfried**, who observed somewhere between four and nine hands in the work (the original Qohelet, a Sadducean deist, someone of the wisdom school and a pious fourth, with a group of up to five responsible for further insertions),[15] and this sort of approach held sway for much of the next half-century.[16]

Despite the difficulty people have experienced in discerning a structure, this need not be a cause of despair. Indeed, for some such as Ellul, that no one is able to find a grand structure is perfectly appropriate: it is integral to how Qohelet will communicate his message, and moreover, what could be more appropriate for a book questioning the meaning of life than to reveal no structure!

2. Collected Aphorisms

Not satisfied with finding no meaning, one response was to read Ecclesiastes in a manner not dissimilar to a common approach to Proverbs; that is, rather than trying to find an extant structure, as wisdom literature it makes sense to systematize the book according to topic by collecting aphorisms which discussed the same topic. One could imagine drawing together sayings on work, on pleasure, on justice, on rulers, on money and so on. Apart from anything else, this adds greatly to the everyday utility of Ecclesiastes,

---

im Kloster war." WA Tischreden 1.207, as cited in Wolters, "Ecclesiastes and the Reformers," 63.

15. Siegfried, *Prediger und Hoheslied*, as quoted in Murphy, *Ecclesiastes*, xxxiv; as well as Longman, *Book of Ecclesiastes*, 11.

16. See the survey of and discussion of this approach in Murphy, *Ecclesiastes*, xxxiii.

PART 1: THE HISTORY OF THE SEARCH FOR A STRUCTURE

making it more accessible and approachable as a source of wisdom for everyday life.

Walther Zimmerli implicitly suggests the potential viability of such an approach with his 1974 article, "Traktat oder Sentenzensammlung?" (Treatise or Sayings-Collection?). Among other things, one key point is that the book could read as either a treatise or a collection of sayings, and one can garner much evidence to support either approach. He notes the presence of many independent sentences as well as smaller collections within the book. He suggests, for instance, that such collecting has taken place in the formation of the book, pointing to the chain of seven טוב-sayings in chapter 7.[17]

In this Zimmerli is consciously building on the work of the source critics who attempt to discern different hands behind different sayings or groups of sayings.[18] Zimmerli sees parallels between Proverbs 10 and Ecclesiastes 7, between Proverbs 30 and Ecclesiastes 3, between Proverbs 22:27ff. and Ecclesiastes 4:17—5:6, as well as between the more story-like wisdom in Proverbs 24:30ff. and the narrative of Ecclesiastes 1:12–15 and 16–18.[19] Zimmerli thus demonstrates the appropriateness of reading Ecclesiastes as wisdom, due to its many parallels with the rich source of wisdom sayings that Proverbs is.

While not advocating such a position, **Ellul**'s approach would also lend itself to such a conclusion. He notes that the book drifts between the three maxims of vanity, wisdom and God, and that it does so via some twenty central themes which have been "deliberately dispers[ed]" throughout the book.[20] These themes include work, happiness, power, money, property, death and language, with much wisdom to be found on these and others besides. And yet Ellul would caution the reader against extracting the aphorisms from their context. Although the reader might be tempted

17. That is, the "better-than" sayings. Zimmerli, "Traktat oder Sentenzensammlung?" 225–26.
18. See the discussion in Bartholomew, *Ecclesiastes*, 75.
19. Zimmerli, "Traktat oder Sentenzensammlung?," 223–25.
20. Ellul, *Reason for Being*, 35.

to systematize these themes for their own purposes, the dense interweaving of thematic strands is Qohelet's way of preventing his words being taken as "just a collection of proverbs, recommendations, and occasional trite sayings."[21]

3. Logical Progression

If Ellul is correct in his warning against systematization of the sayings in Ecclesiastes, then the question could rightly be asked whether we can find any progression or development in Qohelet's thought as the book progresses. That is, why has the author chosen to weave the wisdom throughout the book as they have, rather than grouping it in a way which might better aid the reader? Is there a story which is being told, which might follow the established pattern of a beginning, some form of quest and then a fitting conclusion?

One approach which did read Ecclesiastes in this way comes from **Gregory Thaumaturgus'** early Christian interpretation in his *Metaphrase*. There are very few plot points or evidence of awareness of a structure which might shape the way the story is understood,[22] as he retells the book in his own words, at times paraphrasing, at times interpreting, in what amounts to a stream of consciousness. He evidently sees both the original and his own *Metaphrase* as one continuous monologue through the voice of an elderly and now reflective Solomon.

One might contrast this with **Jerome**, who writes in a manner much more akin to modern commentaries, replete with text-critical comments and scholarly interaction.[23] However, like Gregory Thaumaturgus beforehand, he often paraphrases and rephrases Ecclesiastes and is much more focused on reading Ecclesiastes as

---

21. Ellul, *Reason for Being*, 36.

22. His first and only real note of any awareness of structure comes at the first line of chapter 4, "And leaving all these reflections." Thaumaturgus, "Metaphrase," para. 49459.

23. Jerome, *Commentary on Ecclesiastes*.

PART 1: THE HISTORY OF THE SEARCH FOR A STRUCTURE

a treatise on asceticism, evincing his *contemptus mundi*,[24] which would be the mainstay in Qohelet studies for at least a millennium.[25]

Michael Fox suggests the logical progression in the title of his commentary, *A Time to Tear Down and a Time to Build Up*. That is, despite the "lack of sequential organization," the book drives the reader along, with its two threads of tearing down and building up. Critiquing Wright (see below), he writes, "Wright claims to have solved the Riddle of the Sphinx, but perhaps there is no riddle, no hidden structural code to be 'cracked'. The book does not progress in an organized fashion but rather wanders about, finally leading back (in 12:8) to the starting point."[26] And "[y]et, the book of Qohelet does not lack coherence."[27] That is, while for Fox the structure is neither well articulated nor hierarchical, there is indeed a flow to the book, which might better be described as a "cohesiveness [which] inheres above all in the constant presence of a single brooding consciousness meditating all the book's observations, counsels, and evaluations."[28] It is this consciousness which bids the reader journey along with Qohelet on his project of demolishing and rebuilding meaning.

Most recently, however, **David Beldman** has honed in on the beginning and end of Qohelet's story, framed as it is by the introduction and conclusion (1:1–11 and 12:8–14), but has gone further in drawing attention to the bonus narration found in 7:27, "says Qohelet." This leads Beldman to understand the body of the book as a quest, and by reading it that way feels he is able to account for Qohelet's contradictions, the psychological dimension, and of course, the narrative shape (beginning, middle and end)

---

24. That is, contempt for the world, the foundation of asceticism.

25. Ultimately it was Luther who was the first to properly suggest an optimistic reading, as against Jerome's pessimistic one. However, this is not hugely surprising considering he brewed his own beer and married an ex-nun! See Luther, *Luther's Works*, vol. 15.

26. Fox, *Qohelet and His Contradictions*, 157.

27. Fox, *Qohelet and His Contradictions*, 158.

28. Fox, *A Time*, 151.

9

of Qohelet's quest.²⁹ Qohelet's journey begins with the description of his quest and methodology (1:12–18), the midpoint is marked with his midpoint reflections (7:23–29) and the poem at the end on rejoicing and remembering completes his journey (11:7—12:7).³⁰ The insertion of the narrator provides us with the clues as to how the journey is progressing (or at least the three most critical points of beginning, middle and end), and Beldman sees a "subtle shift" from failed quest in the first two thirds of the book to "expression [. . .] tempered with epistemological humility."³¹

Beldman is to be commended for trying to make sense of the otherwise inexplicable interjection of the narrator's voice in 7:27, and has done a good job in forcing the reader to think about Ecclesiastes along narrative lines, with progression and change in the character of Qohelet. However, despite his very nuanced assessment of his predecessors, Beldman seems to be relying more on intuitions than on cues in the text beyond the occurrences of קהלת (Qohelet), and furthermore his description of the narrative arc is not overly convincing.

4. Keywords

Beldman's identification of קהלת is one example of a keyword to give some shape to the structure of Ecclesiastes, but he is one of many, especially since the 1960s, who think there is a keyword (are keywords) which structures the book into sections. Some of these see their keyword(s) structuring the book as a divider, while others draw attention to the frequency of keyword(s) in some parts rather than others.

Zimmerli identifies occasions where the beginning of the experience narrative is signaled by "die Wahrnehmung" (the perception): ראיתי (I saw), and is followed by "die Schlußfolgerung" (the

---

29. Beldman, "Framed!," 149.
30. Beldman, "Framed!," 154–55.
31. Beldman, "Framed!," 159.

PART 1: THE HISTORY OF THE SEARCH FOR A STRUCTURE

conclusion): ידעתי (I knew).³² He unfortunately only notes several occurrences of these without continuing this analysis throughout the rest of the book, which I have pursued in my analysis below. He has also noted clusters, such as the repeated use of טוב in the טוב-sayings, as noted by Zimmerli above.

A more thorough approach using the concept of keywords is found in a paper by **Giorgio Castellino**, who has some brilliant insights into the structure of the book of Ecclesiastes. Unfortunately his work has been mostly overlooked, not so much because of the quality of his work, but rather due to the relative prominence given to his colleague, Addison Wright, whose hugely influential work happened to appear in the following edition of the *Catholic Bible Quarterly*, and in the same 1968 omnibus of that journal.

Castellino's first important keyword is not so much a word as a verb-form: the first-person verb, which occurs much more regularly until 4:16 and much less afterwards.³³ The first half of the book (1:1—4:16) also contains two thirds of the uses of הבל (vanity), as well as the phrase "chasing or shepherding the wind," plus cognates of עמל (labor). He contrasts this with other phrases such as evil/bad which are more common in the second half.

Another interesting observation is the almost-bookending of the second half with the phrase ירא את־האלהים (fear God), found only in 5:6 [5:7] and 12:13. For Castellino this shows the concerns about הבל (vanity) raised in the first half are given an orthodox assessment in the second.³⁴

Addison G. Wright follows closely on Castellino's heels, and, with much the same broad approach, has produced the most influential and long-lasting structure to date.³⁵ His structure begins

32. Zimmerli, "Prediger," 129.

33. Castellino, "Qohelet and His Wisdom," 17; See also Salyer, *Vain Rhetoric*, 67, who writes of Castellino, "In fact, his is the first study, to my knowledge, that understands how Qoheleth's 'I' directly influences the reader's perception of the structure of the book."

34. Castellino, "Qohelet and His Wisdom," 22. Adding to his thesis, the idea also occurs two further times in the second half (7:18; 8:12), but also once in the first: "God does [it] such that people might fear him" (3:14).

35. Note the comments by Murphy, *Ecclesiastes*, xl, where, despite his

by observing the somewhat regular occurrence of "a chase after wind", although only up to 6:9. The nine occurrences (the double occurrence in 4:4–6 he counts as one) provide Wright with eight sections, and make a larger division of the book into 1:1—6:9 and 6:10—12:14.[36] Wright is able to give some structure to the second half after first discovering the repetition of "do not know" and "no knowledge" in chapters 9–11, while later discovering a pattern of "not find/who can find" for chapters 7–8.[37]

Wright worked tirelessly over the years to demonstrate the validity of his structure as revealed by his chosen theme words. However, as he drilled further down into his structure, in order to give his argument a firmer underpinning, he took a turn down the dubious path of numerology.[38] Graham Ogden summarizes a common response to this shift in Wright's work:

> Subsequent to his earlier attempt, Wright has now advanced a numerical thesis, based on the numerical value of select, though not necessarily key, terms in the book (1980, 1983). His hope is to prove the correctness of his earlier view about the overall structure of the work, but the theory is built upon such an arbitrary use of evidence that one cannot take it seriously.[39]

Unfortunately the path of numerology tends to be a circular one, searching for evidence which supports one's own thesis and disregarding data that would disprove it. Michael Fox in particular is quite scathing, viewing Wright's proposal as "a scaffolding that collapses when posts and cross-beams are removed." Fox goes on to dismantle several of Wright's "cross-beams":[40]

---

numerous criticisms of Wright (for example, "arbitrary flights of fancy"), he nonetheless follows the structure "discovered" by Wright.

36. Wright, "Riddle of the Sphinx," 321.

37. My order of description follows Wright's reported order of discovery in Wright, "Riddle of the Sphinx," 323.

38. See his two follow-up articles: Wright, "Riddle of the Sphinx Revisited" and "Additional Numerical Patterns in Qoheleth."

39. Ogden, *Qoheleth*, 30.

40. Summarised from Fox, *A Time*, 148–49.

PART 1: THE HISTORY OF THE SEARCH FOR A STRUCTURE

1. The "dubious cohesiveness" of the word-groups used to divide units;
2. The relative prominence of words and phrases other than those he has outlined;
3. The randomness of the placement of key phrases, which may or may not be preceded or succeeded by several verses;
4. The mismatch between Wright's plan and Qohelet's thought.

Perhaps most damaging is Fox's conclusion that Wright's "proposed structure has no more effect on interpretation than a ghost in the attic. A literary or rhetorical structure should not merely 'be there'; it must *do* something. It should guide readers in recognizing and remembering the author's train of thought."[41]

Although not overly concerned with structure, **Graham Ogden** decided upon יתרון (gain; 1:3 and seven key usages thereafter) as the keyword around which Qohelet's questions revolve in chapters 1–8.[42] Ogden makes a truly helpful insight about the back-and-forth question-and-answer procedure in this section, as Qohelet tries to work out about what can and cannot be gained. What is not explained is how he justifies the section continuing from chapters 1 to 8, or even to the end of the book, as יתרון does not occur at all in the book after 6:11. So while not dismissing the importance of יתרון for understanding Qohelet's evaluations, and while it may well be thematically important, it is hard to justify identifying this word as the word used to structure this book.

Ogden's identification of יתרון has found one recent adherent, with **Andreas Reinert** identifying these as the "Struktursignale im Text," which he understands to be "deutlich und eindeutig."[43] Noting the fourfold occurrence(s) of מה-יתרון (what gain?), he has identified four verses or sections which ask the "Zentralfrage: Was ist der Gewinn?" (1:3; 3:9–11; 5:15; 6:8,11).[44] However, rather than

---

41. Fox, *A Time*, 148–49. Italics original.
42. Ogden, *Qoheleth*, 14–15, 22–26.
43. Reinert, *Salomofiktion*, 24.
44. Reinert, *Salomofiktion*, 169.

dividing the book into sections, this *Zentralfrage* punctuates the text, governing all of Qohelet's searching and observations which are analyzed in the rest of the body.

Reinert goes on to identify a highly complex structure, of which this reaffirmed *Zentralfrage* plays some role, but also twenty-one "Erkenntniswege," interspersed with six "Programmen," three "Weisheitssprüche," one section of "Paranaesen," as well as the "Äusserer" and "Innerer Rahmen," all of which depend not necessarily on keywords but on his analysis of the role each part plays in explicating the book's quest.

While those surveyed above have described one or more words, **Stephan de Jong** draws attention to the semantic range of those words which are clustered together. He looks, for instance, at those theme words associated with work or labor and where they occur in clusters. He finds that those words occur alongside הבל, as well as Qohelet's enjoyment texts, and he calls those areas "observation complexes."[45]

De Jong's approach has much to commend it. Identifying semantic ranges rather than drilling down on one particular word is a worthy hypothesis to test, and so too grouping together themes which relate to each other makes a lot of sense to me also (for example, the overlapping discussion in Ecclesiastes of הבל, work and enjoyment taking place in the same sections).

5. Paneling

De Jong's observations about keywords continue into an elegant structure,[46] which separates out four panels of observation complexes, revealing four alternate panels of instruction. He explains that his approach identifies two distinct modes of discussion in the book, which he was able to do so by means of his three "intuitions," which are worth repeating here in full:

---

45. Jong, "Book on Labour," 110–11, 115, 116.

46. Adopted without modification, for instance, by Webb, *Five Festal Garments*, 87.

PART 1: THE HISTORY OF THE SEARCH FOR A STRUCTURE

> The first is that we have to start with stylistic and semantic observations. The second is that the structure of the book can only be described adequately if we reckon not only with one structuring principle, but with more. The third intuition is that in structuring the book the writer did not apply modern western standards, such as absolute consistency and systematism. We have to look for principles as applied in the ancient wisdom literature.[47]

His cognizance of the different eras he and the author of Ecclesiastes inhabit means the interpreter has to feel their way around for a structure rather than imposing one which might fit a modern logic but be quite alien to the ancient context.

De Jong confesses that his structure is not perfect, which is explained by his third intuition, that one mustn't expect consistency. His observation and instruction divisions rely on density rather than absolute occurrences, and he admits there is overlap with observation in instruction complexes and vice versa.[48] His best intuition at a structure is as follows:

1:1 Introduction
1:2 Motto

1:3—4:16 Observation complex	4:17—5:8 Instruction complex
5:9—6:9 Observation complex	6:10—7:22 Instruction complex
7:23-29 Observation complex	8:1-8 Instruction complex
8:9—9:12 Observation complex	9:13—12:7 Instruction complex

12:8 Motto
12:9-14 Conclusion

Despite all the impressive points, the single biggest flaw in de Jong's structure comes when one actually tries to read through the book using this structure. There may indeed be densities of instruction or observation that alternate, but unfortunately the many important observations made do not help us read the text better, and

---

47. Jong, "Book on Labour," 107–8.
48. Jong, "Book on Labour," 108.

surely that must be the goal of discerning a structure, as Fox, with reference to Wright, has noted.

Choon-Leong Seow has followed the sense of de Jong's structure by also seeing alternating panels. Although, where de Jong alternated observation with instruction, Seow alternates reflection and ethics, as follows:[49]

> IA Reflection: Everything Is Ephemeral and Unreliable (1:2—4:16)
> IB Ethics: Coping with Uncertainty (4:17—6:9)
> IIA Reflection: Everything is Elusive (6:10—8:17)
> IIB Ethics: Coping with Risks and Death (9:1–10)

Seow perceives a general shift from the indicative to the imperative between the two halves, so that within each half problems are raised which are then resolved: the ethical response to the problem of vanity is how to cope with uncertainty, and elusiveness is answered with teaching on how to cope with the unknown (in particular, risks and death).

As with de Jong, Seow's structure is helpful in reinforcing the to-and-fro nature of Ecclesiastes, where a problem is raised and discussed, solutions proffered and complications considered. Of all the structures considered, Seow's makes the most sense of the style of the book. Like all structures there are problems, not least the material that does not fit his schema. He will summarize, for instance, Qohelet's first reflections (1:2—4:16) as "Everything is Ephemeral and Unreliable," yet Qohelet reflects on things which are neither ephemeral nor unreliable. Similarly, the reflection sections provide ethical implications before the following section, which is supposed to be reserved for ethics. That said, it is disappointing that, to my knowledge, no commentators have yet taken up Seow's structure for themselves, but this perhaps comes back to the question of readability—for all its good points, the structure does not have anything solid to ground it and to excite others to embrace it.

What de Jong and Seow both fail to do is to ground their divisions in specific textual observations. Thus, de Jong can have a

---

49. Seow, *Ecclesiastes*, 47–48.

fluid structure with overlap, and Seow can describe his panels with equivalent terms to de Jong, and this is despite having only half the number of panels. Nonetheless, this does not mean the project of discerning panels in the body of Ecclesiastes must be jettisoned altogether.

As mentioned above, **Zimmerli's** 1974 essay, "Traktat oder Sentenzensammlung," ends up equivocating between the two options of treatise and sayings-collection. The evidence he marshals in favor of the treatise options are those passages in Ecclesiastes akin to Proverbs 24:30–34 and Psalm 37:25, 35ff., which, despite being wisdom literature, contain more story-like elements, are less aphoristic and contain first-person observation.[50] In his 1962 commentary he describes such a section as an "Erlebnisschilderung" (experience narrative).[51]

Disappointingly, Zimmerli's rather unsatisfactory answer is to put it back on the individual reader to decide for themselves what they think it is, either a treatise or a collection of aphorisms. Nonetheless, throughout his essay he is clear there are indeed parts which are to be read more like a narrative (Qohelet's treatise), while there are other parts which are collected aphorisms according to a theme, and the careful exegete must work out which parts are more Job-like and which are more akin to Proverbs.[52] Adapting the title of his essay, my argument is that rather than "Traktat *oder* Sentenzensammlung?" (italics added), Ecclesiastes is better understood as "Traktat *und* Sentenzensammlung."

Drawing These Threads Together

After reviewing the previous approaches, we are in a position to draw out the best threads in the hope of weaving a new approach.

"**Traktat**" ***und*** "**Sentenzensammlung**": The difficulty in classifying Ecclesiastes according to genre, as exemplified by

---

50. Zimmerli, "Traktat oder Sentenzensammlung?," 224.
51. Zimmerli, "Prediger," 129.
52. Zimmerli, "Traktat oder Sentenzensammlung?," 230.

Zimmerli, is that the genre one chooses depends on which section one focuses on to make that decision. It could well be classified as a narrative, with the wisdom illustrating the points made by the narrative. Conversely, it could be classified as wisdom, with the narrative the outworking of the wisdom. The truth of the matter is that both of these genres are present, and rather than choosing one or the other, it is instead more prudent to ask how these two forms of discourse, both narrative and wisdom, are used together in the book, how they work together, and how they play off one another.

Alternation: To state that wisdom and narrative are both present is one thing, but the arrangement of those forms of discourse is ultimately the question of this work. To that end, it is worth drawing attention again to the many interpreters who see alternation in the book, whether in the two-part question-and-answer alternation seen by Castellino and Wright or in the thematic alternation seen by de Jong and Seow. My contention is that the alternation is between the narrative sections and the wisdom sections.

Keywords: The idea of keywords has several adherents, Wright being perhaps chief among them. Yet Wright's keywords are not consistent, and he had to find new keywords for the second half of the book. Similarly, Ogden and Reinert's identification of יתרון serves them well but also fails to account for the larger part of the book. As suggested earlier, all of these keywords could be best described as *thematic* keywords, which are decided upon somewhat a priori. It would seem preferable to find an a posteriori *structural* keyword(s).

Following on from this, my proposal is to combine all three of these approaches in my structure as follows:

Taking our cue from the description in 1:12 which introduces us to Qohelet as observer, we can describe one type of discourse present in Ecclesiastes as first-person narrative, or observation. And taking our cue from the description of Qohelet's work in 12:9–10 as a collector and curator of משלים (proverbs), we can describe the other type of discourse as wisdom. This is quite similar to Zimmerli's "Traktat" and "Sentenzensammlung," and to de

Jong's "Observation" and "Instruction," as well as to Seow's "Reflection" and "Ethics."

Given the recognition of these two types of discourse, the next step is to discern the division between the discourses. The panels of de Jong (as well as Seow) are all well and good, but there are no suggestions of how to draw a line between their panels. De Jong relies on his "intuitions," and while there are clusters of themed vocabulary to give some shape to some of the panels, more can be done in this area, which is where the concept of structural keywords can progress this approach.

As hinted at above, my approach is not to look for a thematic keyword and fit a structure around it, but to look for a structural keyword, which might not present itself beforehand, but makes sense after the fact. One proposal along this line from the New Testament world is the pattern in the book of Romans identified by Richard Gibson and Grant Nichols,[53] where panels *confirming* the gospel alternate with panels *defending* the gospel against Jewish objections. A majority of their panels end with the phrase "(through) Jesus Christ (our) Lord," and furthermore the panels defending the gospel are replete with language reflecting the history of Israel.[54] My point in explaining the approach of Gibson and Nichols is that they first identified (or perhaps intuited!) the concept of panels, but then noticed the keyword (or key phrase) and the role it played in delineating the structure. Their key phrase is not one they began with, but they happened upon it through the process of evaluating the letter, such that only after the fact were they able to comment on the appropriateness of that keyword to the message of Romans. Their approach to the panels reveals structural keywords which make sense only after one discovers the role they play.

---

53. Unpublished, but adopted for the recent commentary by Peterson, *Commentary on Romans*.

54. Similar points could be made about Richard Bauckham's James structure based around his identification of sections beginning with "(my) brothers and sisters." Bauckham, *James*. Furthermore, one might also note the shaping of the structure of the book of Acts around the phrase noting the "spread" of "the word of the Lord."

My structure takes up these three concepts, with the structure of alternating panels delineated by the occurrence of ראה (to see, and especially the first-person *qatal* and *yiqtol* ראיתי/אראה, I saw), which gives shape to the panels of observation, and these panels alternate with panels of collected wisdom.

The key points in the structure which I will demonstrate below can be summarized as follows:

1. In the body of the book there are four pairs of alternating panels.
2. They are delineated by the keyword ראה (especially the first-person ראיתי/אראה).
3. This keyword provides internal organization to those panels.
4. These panels alternate with panels of collected aphorisms.
5. The pairs of observation and wisdom panels explicate the same theme according to their genre.

I will explain how this comes about in detail in what follows, but in order to preview the discussion to come I will present my structure in outline here for reference. In Part 2 I will explain the structure of the observation panels in detail, showing how ראה is used to provide the internal organization to the panels. It is fair to say that my structure bears many similarities to de Jong's, although my divisions are grounded not so much in intuitions as in textual observations based around the verb ראה. I have also highlighted the opening and closing poems as a key part of the book's structure (which bears some conceptual resemblance to Reinert's concept of "Rahmen," albeit with different contents). My own structure then is as follows:

PART 1: THE HISTORY OF THE SEARCH FOR A STRUCTURE

1:1–2 Introduction to Qohelet's Words

1:3–11 Opening Poem

1:12—2:26 Observation Panel	3:1–9 Wisdom Collection
3:10—4:16 Observation Panel	4:17—5:11 Wisdom Collection
5:12—6:12 Observation Panel	7:1–14 Wisdom Collection
7:15—9:13 Observation Panel	9:14—11:6 Wisdom Collection

11:7—12:7 Concluding Poem

12:8-14 Conclusion to Qohelet's words

Why ראה?

So, why ראה? This is not an intuitive thematic keyword, nor has it been previously examined (to my knowledge) as a potential keyword. As with Gibson and Nichols, this was an a posteriori observation which came out of an heuristic process, rather than an a priori exploration as some have attempted, for example, with more suggestive keywords like הבל, with a post hoc structure fitted to them.

Now of course it would be nice if Ecclesiastes had been passed down by its author with chapter headings or a table of contents, making this project redundant. But as with all literary structures which are not explicitly noted by the author, the process of determining a structure must needs be a largely heuristic endeavor. In the same way as genre is largely inductively determined, noting cues and patterns and vocabulary and phrasing, so too does the reading and rereading of the text suggest certain patterns and organizing principles. It is such a recursive process which suggests which clues are to be noted, to be incorporated into reading other parts of the text, and cause other parts to be reread, paying attention to cues not noted in prior readings.

This is a process which has been undertaken in other literature from a similar milieu, as evidenced in John Harvey's *Listening to the Text: Oral Patterning in Paul's Letters*. Although the majority of the book discusses the *Hauptbriefe* of Paul, he predicates part of his work on the discussion of two types of echoing present in

Homer's *Odyssey*. The first type of echoing he finds in 5.225–48, where he demonstrates Homer's repetition of lexemes and short phrases to tie sections together.[55] Reusing a phrase or repeating the same or similar vocabulary orients the listener so they know that the same topic is under discussion.

With regards to the second type of echoing, Harvey, following Whitman, notes the use of γινώσκω on either side of a seventy-five-line interlude (19.392–94, 464–68) to bring the reader back as the main narrative is resumed.[56] "Homer thus uses repeated wording to give his listeners a means of following the main story line."[57] Harvey explains that "such echoes may well extend over multiple sections of a given work."[58] He notes that:

> in the case of Hebrew poetry ... synonyms were frequently used to continue a theme over an extended portion of a composition ... Furthermore, the fact that scholars have noted the presence of both inclusion and ring-composition in the OT ... suggests that Jewish composers recognized the value of repeated wording to structure longer sections of their compositions.[59]

I am arguing here that ראה plays a very similar role in Ecclesiastes. When Qohelet wants the reader to heed his observations he draws their attention to it through ראיתי/אראה. The natural question is "whether the audience, listening to an aural presentation ... could possibly have caught signs of such 'fearful symmetry,' or whether it would have meant anything to them if they did."[60] Whitman's response to his own question is that "the human mind is a strange organ, and one which perceives many things without

---

55. Harvey, *Listening to the Text*, 57–58.

56. Harvey, *Listening to the Text*, 58–59; engaging with Whitman, *Homer and the Heroic Tradition*.

57. Harvey, *Listening to the Text*, 59.

58. Harvey, *Listening to the Text*, 59; discussing Havelock, "Alphabetization of Homer," 14.

59. Harvey, *Listening to the Text*, 59.

60. Harvey, *Listening to the Text*, 59; quoting Whitman, *Homer and the Heroic Tradition*, 255.

PART 1: THE HISTORY OF THE SEARCH FOR A STRUCTURE

conscious or articulate knowledge of them, and responds to them with emotions necessarily and appropriately vague. An audience hence might feel more symmetry than it could possibly analyze or describe."[61] Such an understanding of the literary milieu of the Greek-speaking world, at least between Homer and the New Testament era (which more than adequately encompasses the majority's post-exilic dating of Ecclesiastes), means that such an approach has merits in helping us understand the structure of Ecclesiastes. The use of ראיתי/אראה as a keyword throughout the book serves as a verbal hook to remind the reader, especially after hearing sections of Qohelet's collected wisdom, that they are now hearing Qohelet's observations.

Despite the different languages, the common literary milieu of *Odyssey* and Ecclesiastes means it should not be unusual to expect this sort of literary patterning in Ecclesiastes. In particular, this includes these traits of repetition within sections and resumptive keywords or phrases extended over larger units, or indeed the whole book. Whether for the purposes of memorization or for aiding the expected audience of listeners rather than readers in a culture without as much access to writings as today, authors aid their audiences through the use of these features.

All that being said, the determining of a structure remains an organic, heuristic, recursive process. Nonetheless, I will attempt to describe the logic behind my own process of deciding upon this structure. I will try to explain the process of noting clues and recursive reading as well as what that says about how the reader is to position themselves within the text. In one sense, what follows is unimportant; what matters is whether the final structure "works." But in another sense, the process of uncovering is just as important as what is arrived at, lest the final structure simply be an arbitrary intuiting neither coming out of, nor helping to make sense of, the text.

---

61. Whitman, *Homer and the Heroic Tradition*, 255; in Harvey, *Listening to the Text*, 59.

SEEING WHAT QOHELET SAW

1. Observation of seams in the first three chapters

The book of Ecclesiastes opens with a narrator's introduction to Qohelet (1:1-2), followed by a poem (1:3-11), then a reintroduction to Qohelet by Qohelet in the first-person (1:12-13). After a description of his conative attempts to find meaning through exploits, at the beginning of chapter 3 a seam is evident with another poem. This reveals at least three parts to the book: 1:1-11; 1:12—2:26; 3:1ff. These sections could also be described, respectively, as general third-person observations, specific first-person observations and general third-person observations.

2. First-person verbs describe Qohelet's observations

On closer examination, the second section (1:12—2:26), which begins with Qohelet introducing himself (1:12-13, in contrast to the narrator's introduction to him in 1:1-2), is replete with first-person singular verbs. In only thirty-three verses there are forty-five first-person singular verbs. The verbs here describe both the activities of Qohelet as well as his opinion of the value of those activities.

The primary verb of observation is ראה, and it occurs in the first person as either ראיתי or אראה at regular intervals throughout this first section (1:14; 2:3, 13, 24). But beyond this verb, it is worth noting the other first-person verbs in this panel. They could be grouped into four groups of verbs of exploration, excelling, achievement and also failure. The first group of verbs are נתן (1:13, 17), דבר (1:16), נסה (2:1), תור (2:3), אמר (2:1, 2, 15), ידע (1:17; 2:14), פנה (2:11, 12), which describe Qohelet's decisions to explore. A further group of verbs reflect Qohelet's positive self-evaluation, where גדל (1:16; 2:4, 9), יסף (1:16; 2:9) and חכם (2:15, 18) note his excellence. The next set describe what was or was not done, with (לא) אצל (2:8), כנס (2:7), קנה (2:5, 6, 8), עשה (2:4, 5), נטע (2:4), בנה (2:10), מנע (לא) (2:10) and עמל (2:11, 18, 20), while a final group reflect on Qohelet's ultimate failure to have a lasting achievement,

PART 1: THE HISTORY OF THE SEARCH FOR A STRUCTURE

with שׂנא (2:17, 18), נוח (2:18) and סבב (2:20). Clearly then, the author of Ecclesiastes portrays Qohelet's quest for meaning, at least in this first section, through Qohelet's first-person description and discussion.

My instinct in reading this first section is that the uniqueness of the proliferation of first-person verbs in this first section also reveals one of the keys to the structure. The verbs for exploring occur in several clusters, but no one verb alone reveals any kind of structure. The verbs for excelling are more suggestive of a structure if we were to look at them as a kind of semantic domain (1:16, 16; 2:4, 9, 9, 15, 18), but no verb individually serves this task. The verbs of achievement occur irregularly, and the verbs describing Qohelet's failure are toward the end. Only the single verb for observation, ראה, occurs with anything approaching regularity. Again, it is noteworthy that ראיתי/אראה occurs four times, with fairly even spacing, throughout this section (1:14; 2:3, 13, 24).

3. REGULARITY OF ראה IN THIS PASSAGE

The most prolific first-person verbs in this passage are ראה (4x), followed by אמר, גדל, עמל and עשׂה (3x), while the most prolific verbs here (regardless of person and *binyan*) are עשׂה (11x), היה (9x), ראה (8x), נתן (7x) and ידע (5x). Of these, of note is the regularity of ראה. While the other verbs are clustered or simply too sparse, the verb ראה occurs four times in the first-person with some regularity and spacing. Adding in the other declensions of ראה, it often occurs in pairs (2:1, 3; 2:12, 13; 2:24a, 24b). The same cannot be said for the other verbs in the passage, which do not seem to play any structural role.

4. REGULARITY OF ראה IN OTHER SECTIONS

Chasing this observation made in chapters 1–2 throughout the rest of the book, it is evident that this verb regularly punctuates the text, occurring forty-seven times in the book, with twenty-one of those as a first-person verb. There are occasional absences, but it is never absent for too long. After those occurrences already noted in the first two chapters, it also occurs as a first-person verb at 3:10, 16, 22; 4:1, 4, 7, 15; 5:12[13], 17[18]; 6:1; 7:15; 8:9, 10, 17; 9:13; 10:5, 7. There are no first-person verbs in the final two chapters, although that is not hugely surprising, as the contents of a poem and the conclusion about Qohelet do not contain Qohelet's first-person observations.

5. ראה IS FOUND IN NARRATIVE SECTIONS

When focusing in on those uses of ראה to see whether similar patterns of observation can be observed as were seen in 1:12—2:26, it seems that sections of narrative coincide with occurrences of ראיתי/אראה and often coincide with the beginnings of narrative description of Qohelet's observations in the first person. For instance, 3:10 introduces what Qohelet sees:

> **I saw** [ראיתי] the business which God gave to people to be busy with. He has made everything beautiful in its time. He has also placed eternity in their hearts, such that people are unable to discover the works God has made from beginning to end. (3:10–11)

A similar introduction can also be observed in 3:16:

> And **I saw** [ראיתי] something else under the sun: the place of justice—there was wickedness, and the place of righteousness—there was wickedness. I said to myself, God shall judge the righteous and the wicked, because there is a fitting time for everything, and a time for every deed. (3:16–17)

Qohelet thus continues to observe, continues to describe, as well as to reflect on what he is seeing "under the sun."

One further example for now is this, from chapter 5:

> There is an evil sickness **I saw** [ראיתי] under the sun: wealth guarded to the harm of its owner, and that wealth

PART 1: THE HISTORY OF THE SEARCH FOR A STRUCTURE

perished through a wicked business, such that the child he begets has nothing to inherit. (5:12–13 [13–14])

My argument in this book is that this pattern continues throughout Ecclesiastes, with ראיתי/אראה regularly introducing or concluding the observations of Qohelet, and that these appear in sections of narrative observation. Put more explicitly, I am suggesting that the author has deliberately structured Qohelet's observations around this verb, and by following the outline of Ecclesiastes revealed by this verb we will more closely be able to follow the argument in Ecclesiastes.

6. Clustered aphorisms

If ראיתי/אראה regularly begins sections of narrative, then it is worth considering what precedes them. Continuing with the example of 5:12–13 mentioned above, the occurrence in 5:12 of ראיתי follows this group of aphorisms:

> The lover of silver is never sated with silver,
>   and whoever loves their wealth is not [sated] with their income.
>   This too is meaningless.
> When good things multiply, so too do those who eat them multiply,
>   and what does it profit their owner except to behold them with their eyes?
> Sweet is the sleep of the laborer, whether little or much should they eat,
>   but the abundance of the rich, there is for them no rest for sleep.
> (5:9–11[10–12])

There are examples here of synonymous and antithetical parallelism, which bear a stark contrast to the first-person observations which immediately follow. Similar observations can be made throughout the book, with the wisdom poem in 3:1–9 preceding the observations beginning at 3:10, as well as those wisdom sayings in chapter 7 which lead up to the section of Qohelet's observations which begin at 7:15 (את־הכל ראיתי). Immediately following these clusters of aphorisms, ראיתי invariably reappears as a verbal hook to signal to the listener that they are again in a part of Ecclesiastes where Qohelet is narrating his observations (see also especially 3:10; 5:12; 7:15).

Summary

My observations about the first-person use of ראה in Ecclesiastes would seem to be fairly unique in ancient Near Eastern wisdom literature, although "[a]ll Egyptian Wisdom Instructions... present themselves as the teaching of individuals." Nonetheless the character of the sage usually "disappears almost entirely," while what Qohelet sees and his continual self-reflection in Ecclesiastes "goes far beyond its predecessors in the importance it gives to the organizing consciousness of the sage."[62] In his earlier work Fox points to several Egyptian wisdom writings, as well as, interestingly, Deuteronomy and Tobit as illustrations of the frame narrator presenting the wisdom of the sage.[63] None of these works are as committed to the first-person narrative as is Qohelet, but the model is certainly there in other ancient Near Eastern literature for the author of Ecclesiastes to follow and develop. So while Ecclesiastes may well be unique, this observation is by no means controversial. Rather, the way Qohelet's observations are written fits soundly within the technique of other ancient Near Eastern wisdom literature.

What is unique in my approach to the structure is maintaining that the first-person narration based around the observations of the main character does not only typify Ecclesiastes but more importantly also structures Ecclesiastes.

The observations made here about the verb ראה and its use by the author of Ecclesiastes to structure the narrative of Qohelet can only be maintained if they make better sense of the flow and arguments of the book than other structures, and must ultimately be seen to be believed. The proof must be in the pudding, because, to quote Michael Fox again, any "proposed structure [must have]

---

62. Fox, *Qohelet and His Contradictions*, 159.
63. Fox, "Frame-Narrative and Composition," 92–94.

PART 1: THE HISTORY OF THE SEARCH FOR A STRUCTURE

more effect on interpretation than a ghost in the attic. A literary or rhetorical structure should not merely 'be there'; it must *do* something. It should guide readers in recognizing and remembering the author's train of thought."[64] My sincere hope is that the structure presented in this book does precisely that.

In Part 2 I will detail how both the observation panels stand out from the wisdom collections, as well as the internal structure of the observation panels. My hope is that thereby the validity of such an approach to this book will be demonstrated. In Part 3 I will discuss the wisdom collections and their relationship to the observation panels. Finally, in Part 4 I will look at the internal and external bookends, namely, the opening and closing poems and the introduction and conclusion to Qohelet's words.

---

64. Fox, *A Time*, 148–49.

PART 2: The Observation Panels

Observation Panels in Summary

What I have been arguing about the observation panels is essentially this: the author of Ecclesiastes has deliberately used the verb ראה to indicate to the reader those places where Qohelet details his observations, both the boundaries of the wider sections, as well as the internal structure to these sections. As they are the observations of Qohelet, who speaks in the first person, more often than not it will be either ראיתי/אראה, that is, the first-person *qatal* or *yiqtol* form of the verb ראה (to see). My contention is that this verb begins all the units of observation, and in roughly half the cases it also concludes those units.[1] For clarity's sake, this is how I will describe the parts of Ecclesiastes according to this structure:

1. "Panel" describes a concentration of Qohelet's observation or of his wisdom (e.g., 1:12—2:26).

2. "Unit" describes those subdivisions of the observation panels which are signaled by the author's placements of ראה (e.g., 1:12–18).

---

1. It is also worth briefly stating that ראה does not have to be the absolute first or last word in a unit, but that its presence in a section identifies that section as the beginning or end of a unit and/or panel. See also my earlier comments regarding the pattern seen in *Odyssey*.

PART 2: THE OBSERVATION PANELS

3. "Section" describes the smaller parts of a unit (e.g., 1:12-13), so that we have panel > unit > section.

Following this language, Ecclesiastes contains four observation panels, each based around the verb ראה, with, respectively, four, four, three and five units per panel, as outlined below. There are usually four sections in each unit, and they tend to be structured in a concentric ABB`A` pattern.

Panel 1 (1:12—2:26) has four units. They detail Qohelet's observations beginning with ראיתי/אראה and are each preceded by a short preface. The first unit (1:12-18) is prefaced with a reintroduction to the person of Qohelet (1:12-13), while the other three units are prefaced with a short statement which includes another form of the verb ראה which is not ראיתי/אראה. The four units of the first panel are: 1:12-18; 2:1-11; 2:12-23; and 2:24-26.

Panel 2 (3:10—4:16) also has four units, all of which begin with ראיתי/אראה, and all but the first conclude with ראיתי. This second panel also contains an interesting wisdom interlude (4:5-6) between the third and fourth units of the panel, which will be discussed in detail below. The four units of the second panel are: 3:10-15; 3:16-22; 4:1-4; and 4:7-16.

Panel 3 (5:12—6:12) has three units which each begin with ראיתי. This panel stands apart from the others in how its units work together as an ABA` structure. The three units of panel three are: 5:12-16; 5:17-19; and 6:1-12.

Panel 4 (7:15—9:13) is the longest of the observation panels with five units beginning *and* ending with a form of ראה. The first-person ראיתי continues to be used in beginning *or* concluding statements, but other inflections of ראה are used to form the corresponding bookend in each respective unit. The five units of the fourth panel are: 7:15-28; 7:29—8:9; 8:10-16; 8:17—9:10; and 9:11-13.

These four observation panels and the units within them can be represented in the following way:

SEEING WHAT QOHELET SAW

Panel 1	Panel 2	Panel 3	Panel 4
1:12–18	3:10–15	5:12–16	7:15–28a
2:1–11	3:16–21	5:17–19	7:28b—8:9
2:12–23	4:1–4	6:1–12	8:10–16
2:24–26	4:7–16		8:17—9:10
			9:11–13

In Part 3 I will detail the wisdom collection panels which alternate with these observation panels, as well as discussing the relationship between the alternating observation and wisdom panels.

Observation Panels in Detail

Observation Panel 1 (1:12—2:26)

The book opens with an introduction to Qohelet in the third person (1:1–2), then a poem (1:3–11)[2], and then in 1:12–13 Qohelet introduces himself in the first person and describes the basic contours of the journey he is about to embark upon. He is described variously throughout the book, as both a king (1:12) and in sage-like terms (12:9), while the similarity of the introductions to this book and several of the prophets could suggest the author intended Qohelet to be understood as among the prophets.[3] Perhaps the most accurate methodological description of Qohelet, at least in the observation panels, is that he is a surveyor, as he observes the failures and successes of those seeking to live wisely in God's world.[4] This reintroduction to Qohelet begins an observation pan-

---

2. See Part 4 as I examine the bookends to Ecclesiastes.

3. The book opens with "the words of Qohelet the son of David" (דברי קהלת בן־דוד), which is intriguingly similar to the opening of Jeremiah (דברי ירמיהו בן־חלקיהו) and Amos (דברי עמוס); Nehemiah begins in the same fashion also (דברי נחמיה בן־חכליה). A similar construction is also present for the דבר־יהוה which came to Hosea the son of Beeri, to Joel the son of Pethuel, to Micah the Moreshethite and to Zephaniah the son of Cushi. This will be discussed in Part 4.

4. We could also say that Qohelet is not so much a seer (a prophet) as a see-er (an observer).

PART 2: THE OBSERVATION PANELS

el where Qohelet's first-person observations take the reader along with him on his journey to discover meaning in, and even despite, the vanity experienced in life. The furthest limit of this panel is perhaps the most widely agreed boundary in the book, with the wisdom poem on time (beginning at 3:1) signaling the beginning of the following panel.

As the shape of units within this first panel will govern the shape of the rest of the book, it is important to understand what is uniquely happening in this panel as well as what will carry through to the rest of the book. After Qohelet introduces himself and his methodology (1:12–13), Qohelet begins to detail his observations and discussions with the book's first occurrence of ראיתי (1:14). He discusses what he has seen—"all the deeds done under the sun"—and the difficulty of finding sufficient wisdom to comprehend the meaning behind them. Following this, the *yiqtol* form of the verb occurs, as Qohelet wants to see (אראה) what is good for people to do (2:3). The next occurrence of ראיתי (2:13) is part of a new unit which begins at 2:12, signaled by turning (פנה) and considering/evaluating (ראה) wisdom, madness and folly (2:12). In 2:13 the means of consideration is again observation, as Qohelet observes (ראיתי) how wisdom is superior to folly. A conclusion comes at the end of the chapter, as Qohelet has seen (ראיתי) a better option, namely, enjoying the fruits of one's God-given labor (2:24).

This first panel of four units has a regular structure. Each has a brief preface to focus the reader on the observations which follow, and, as with the other panels, the beginning of each unit is signaled by ראיתי/אראה. In the first unit this preceding thought is Qohelet's self-introduction, while in the other three units another declension of ראה prefaces the observation, as follows:

1:12–13 begins this panel by reintroducing Qohelet the observer, with his observations proper beginning in 1:14 with ראיתי:

1:12 אני קהלת הייתי מלך על־ישראל בירושלם:
1:13 ונתתי את־לבי לדרוש ולתור בחכמה על כל־אשר נעשה תחת השמים [. . .]:
1:14 ראיתי את־כל־המעשים שנעשו תחת השמש [. . .]

2:1–2, signaled with וראה, prefaces the observation which begins in 2:3 with אראה:

2:1 אמרתי אני בלבי לכה־נא אנסכה בשמחה וראה בטוב [. . .]:
2:3 תרתי בלבי למשוך ביין את־בשרי ולבי נהג בחכמה ולאחז בסכלות
עד אשר־אראה אי־זה טוב לבני האדם אשר יעשו תחת השמים
מספר ימי חייהם:

2:12, signaled with לראות, prefaces the observation which begins in 2:13 with וראיתי:

2:12 ופניתי אני לראות חכמה והוללות וסכלות [. . .]:
2:13 וראיתי אני שיש יתרון לחכמה מן־הסכלות כיתרון האור מן־החשך:

2:24a–b, signaled with והראה (a third-person masculine singular *hiphil weqatal*), is the preface to the concluding observation (2:24c) of this opening panel, signaled with ראיתי.

2:24 אין־טוב באדם
שיאכל ושתה והראה את־נפשו טוב בעמלו
גם־זה ראיתי אני כי מיד האלהים היא:

If, as I argue, ראיתי/אראה is indeed the key structural marker of this book, then the pattern of this panel in preceding Qohelet's observations by means of these prefaces helps draw attention to the observations which follow and begin with ראיתי/אראה. In this panel the observations are prefaced either by reintroducing the author (1:12–13) or by reminding the reader that this is Qohelet's internal discussion and deliberation (2:1–2), with a reminder of the purpose of these investigations (2:12) or with a summary conclusion (2:24a–b).

This pattern is unique to the first panel; this pattern of a preface does not recur elsewhere in the book. It seems that the reason for this unique structure is to teach the reader to become attuned to ראיתי/אראה signaling the structure. After this first panel the reader is able to find the units without the need for a preface, which explains the more straightforward structure in the other three panels, where ראה is used only to begin and (often) to end

PART 2: THE OBSERVATION PANELS

units rather than to doubly signal their beginning, via a preface and then an introduction proper, as has been the pattern here.

Following this plan, this first observation panel consists of four units, with the final unit acting as a coda or conclusion before a new panel begins at 3:1.[5]

1:12–18 I saw the vanity of work (ראיתי at 1:14)

2:1–11 I saw the vanity of achievement (אראה at 2:3)

2:12–23 I saw the vanity of inheritance (ראיתי at 2:13)

2:24–26 I saw two ways to work (ראיתי at 2:24c)

1:12–18

The unit begins with a discussion of Jerusalem and its king, with all that entails. Qohelet's purpose is to examine what can be known about God's domain. He constantly contrasts what can be known under the sun (תחת השמש)[6]—the limits of human knowledge[7]—and what can be understood about the bigger picture of life under the heavens (תחת השמים)[8]—the bigger perspective visible in its entirety only to God.[9] In 1:13 he proposes to investigate the greater, but he has only access to the lesser. In that respect, we should expect any theology derived from Qohelet's observations to be a bottom-up theology, an experiential one, and the tensions throughout the book will be between what Qohelet has seen and what he knows, or between natural and special revelation.

---

5. See also below where 9:11–13 plays a similar role in the final observation panel.

6. This construction twenty-nine times in the book, although depending on what one believes the referent of the final suffix in 4:15 on תחת to be and how one understands the parallelism in that verse, there may well be an implied thirtieth.

7. "Qoheleth's favourite term for this-worldly experience." Ogden, *Qoheleth*, 30.

8. This construction only thrice in the book: here, 2:3 and 3:1.

9. "[T]his is a reference to all human activity rather than situations in the natural world[.]" Ogden, *Qoheleth*, 34.

The first part of the structure in this first unit is a resumptive introduction to Qohelet. Where he was introduced in the third person in 1:1-2, he now presents himself in the first person (1:12-13). He reminds the reader of his immense resources, with which he intends to attack the problem of vanity, being the king over Israel in Jerusalem. He makes this search his whole purpose, to seek out and explore what wisdom might reveal about the fullness of all of life under the heavens. This introduction leads into the method of Qohelet's search, namely his observations, beginning in 1:14, of this world and all work that is undertaken under the sun.

> Preface: I, Qohelet, set out to understand the burden of life under the heavens. (1:12-13)
>> A **I saw** (ראיתי) the deeds done under the sun were vanity and a chasing after the wind (1:14-15)
>>> B My heart has seen much wisdom (1:16)
>>> B` I gave my heart over to understand wisdom (1:17a)
>> A` I concluded that this experiment was a chasing after the wind (1:17b-18)

As noted by Zimmerli, ראיתי (1:14) and ידעתי (1:17b) often work together in explaining Qohelet's observations and conclusions.[10] After the preface (1:12-13), the two A sections begin with each of these options: what Qohelet observes (ראיתי in 1:14) is then evaluated (ידעתי in 1:17b). In both sections we see the parallel use of the "chasing after the wind" phrase. There is also an interesting double expression in both sections:

1:15	1:18
what is crooked cannot be straight	from wisdom comes sorrow
what is lacking cannot be counted	from knowledge comes grief

In both instances these double expressions express an observed frustration, where the process of making something right is

---

10. Zimmerli, "Prediger," 129.

frustrated, just as those things which should normally yield positives bring about only negative results.

In the B sections we see two other parallel expressions. In both Qohelet addresses his heart as the center of his pursuit, and in both he points to his achievements in wisdom.

What we have then in this first unit is a preface followed by an ABB`A` structure. So far Qohelet's investigations into the deeds done under the heavens, despite his great wisdom, have revealed only that the world does not work as it should. The results of seeking to bring positive change in the world are frustrated, as are the two cure-alls of wisdom and knowledge. His pursuit so far is likened to the vain attempt to shepherd the wind.

In undertaking this search, it is important for Qohelet to assert the breadth of the resources available to him. His resources and the many experiences he shares throughout the book tell the reader that Qohelet (at least in the first two chapters) wants us to see him as a king who is like—or even greater than—Solomon; he is one who has seen all things under the sun and has seen that they are a vanity and a chasing after the wind (1:12–14). This is reiterated in Qohelet's conclusion to this first unit, where his experiences have enabled him to know (ידעתי) that the things of this life, not to mention this entire search, are a chasing after the wind, for wisdom only increases sorrow, and knowledge increases grief (1:17b–18).

Discovering that success is not the result of his endeavors produces a further tension, similar to the way the book began: the words of Qohelet, son of King David in Jerusalem, with all the resources and wisdom available to his station, are nonetheless spoken into a world where everything is vanity (1:1–2). This also provides an introduction to the rest of the panel, where his resources are put to the test, first with pleasure and achievement (2:1–11) and then with the succession *Gedankenexperiment* (2:12–23).

But for now the question is about work, which Qohelet will return to throughout the book. He explores all that is done (נעשׂה 2:13), he looks at all the work that is done (את־כל־המעשׂים שׁנעשׂו 2:14), and interrogates these activities with wisdom, that he might understand the purpose of working under the sun, as he considers all that is done under the heavens. In particular, he seeks to understand what can be good for a person if God has laid such a burden upon them.[11]

2:1-11

If wisdom produces sorrow and knowledge leads to grief, then perhaps there is a different way, as Qohelet outlines in 2:1-11. Just as Qohelet's heart has seen much wisdom and knowledge (1:16), now he will test that wisdom and knowledge, that his heart may see what is good (2:1).

The specific observations in this unit are hedonistically primed; his heart is given wine and folly so he might see what is good. Only then is Qohelet able to observe (אראה) the goodness or otherwise of pleasure (2:3) to determine whether pleasure is indeed good or simply a further instantiation of הבל.

This unit begins and ends with the knowledge that his testing is futile, as laughter and pleasure are madness and produce nothing lasting (2:2). But whether momentary joys or lasting achievements (from a human perspective, cf. 1:4), these are not ultimate "goods," but are fleeting (2:11). This reveals another preface followed by an ABB`A` structure:

Preface: I wanted my heart **to see** (וראה) what is good (2:1-2)

    A **I saw** (אראה) whether pleasure is good under the heavens (2:3)

        B I became great in Jerusalem through my exploits (2:4-8)

        B` I became the greatest in Jerusalem (2:9)

    A` I tried pleasure and gained nothing under the sun (2:10-11)

In the preface to this second unit Qohelet will again see what is good, and while laughter is madness (2:2), he will find out what role pleasure might play in his investigations. It is again his heart

---

11. עִנְיָן (1:13), forming an *inclusio* with 2:26.

PART 2: THE OBSERVATION PANELS

which is the center of his investigations, occurring in the preface (2:1), and in each A section (2:3, 10).

His investigations proper begin with the pleasures of wine and folly, so that he could see (עד אשר־אראה) what was good (2:3). He describes the beginning of his investigations by stating positively that his heart embraces (אחז), and ends them in 2:10 by stating the same idea negatively, with not refusing it (לא אצל). It began with observing and similarly concluded with turning (ופניתי) toward all the deeds his hand had done (cf. 1:14). עשה occurs in both A sections: Qohelet wanted to see what was good for people to *do* (2:3), and then he looked at all his own hands had *done* (2:11).

The two B sections are unequal in length, but nonetheless there is a clear comparison between the two. In the first Qohelet explains he caused great works (הגדלתי מעשי, 2:4), while in the second he simply concludes that he had become great (וגדלתי, 2:9). The first is a catalogue of increasing greatness, all centered around Jerusalem, and compared with others in Jerusalem beforehand (2:7). This comparison is repeated in 2:9 to complete the parallelism, with only a change in number in the verb (than everyone/ than anyone):

2:7 מכל שהיו לפני בירושלם
2:9 מכל שהיה לפני בירושלם

The second unit follows the first in a preface followed by an ABB`A` structure, although אראה is embedded in the opening section rather than fronting it. Pleasure is the focus, as noted twice with שמחה in the preface, then through the picture of wine and folly, and then in the summary with שמחה again (2:10). This pursuit of pleasure is intertwined in the B sections with other pursuits of greatness (2:4–8), culminating in the pleasures of the flesh (2:8), with the reminder that Qohelet's exploits are the greatest of anyone beforehand in Jerusalem (2:7, 9).

The idea here resonates with the imagery of vain "filling" (מלא) in 1:8–9. Qohelet tries to fill himself with pleasurable experiences, first positively (all embracing) and then negatively (not rejecting anything). He has all the resources one could want, more livestock and more extensive output than any of his predecessors (2:7, 9). Toward the center of the unit the list of seven projects is framed with greatness—the greatness of the projects and the resulting greatness of the project manager. The list seems to be of ever increasing value, although the ultimate payoff is inverse, with increasing pleasure and achievements unfortunately resulting only in increasing vanity. Qohelet wanted to see if pursuing pleasure and accruing possessions and achievements would lead to a lasting meaning, and the results of his observations are again negative.

2:12–23

Qohelet's test case in this third unit is inheritance. The question is whether there is any advantage to working for the benefit of one's successor if there is no way of guaranteeing the character of the one who will inherit. It is natural that this question comes to mind after discussing the great projects Qohelet undertook. If there is no advantage in the projects themselves, then what about undertaking them for the advantage of one's descendants?

The introduction to this unit has Qohelet turning to observe (ופניתי אני לראות) wisdom, madness and folly, again in the guise of the person who comes after the king (cf. 1:1, 12). With that introduction, Qohelet discusses his observations, beginning with the orthodox truth that there is more to be gained in wisdom than in folly (2:13).

> Preface: **I looked** (לראות) at wisdom, madness and folly as the successor to the king (2:12)
>> A **I saw** (וראיתי) that wisdom is greater than folly, but that this too is vanity (2:13–15)
>>> B The wise and the fool will die, which is vanity, so I hated life (2:16–17)
>>> B' I hated life because you can't pick who will be wise or a fool, which is vanity (2:18–19)
>> A' I despaired over all of this, and this too is vanity (2:20–23)

PART 2: THE OBSERVATION PANELS

The third unit also has an ABB`A` structure after the preface. The idea of fate runs through the passage, although the root קרה (to befall) appears only in 2:14 and 15 (both times in the same pattern of the noun מקרה (fate) preceding the *yiqtol* of the verb קרה, with at least one word in between). But the idea of being out of control is also present in 2:18 and 21 through the idea of inheritance, where, by definition, one has lost all control.

The first section begins with ראיתי and continues with the twofold use of ידעתי (2:13, 14; cf. 1:14, 17), following Zimmerli's pattern of observation and evaluation as noted above.[12] The first A section contains three comparisons, while the second A section juxtaposes groups of synonyms:

2:13-14	2:20-23
wisdom versus folly	wisdom, knowledge, skill
light versus darkness	vanity and a great evil
wise with eyes versus fools in the dark	toil and anxious striving
	grief and pain

In contrast, the B sections are less colorful, as they both discuss what it is Qohelet hates. In 2:17 Qohelet concludes that he hates life, while in 2:18 he goes into detail about what he hates. In both instances the result is vanity (2:17, 19). The way work is described in 2:17 is through the double use of עשה (to work), and this is paralleled through the similar double use of עמל (toil) in 2:18. In both verses this עשה/עמל is the object of Qohelet's hatred.

Furthermore, in both B sections there is also the note of human ignorance, for as there will be no memory in the future of either the wise or the fool (2:16), neither will there be knowledge in the present of whether one's descendant will be wise or a fool (2:19).

The third unit has the one who follows the king considering the relative merits of wisdom (2:12). Although he observed the preference of wisdom over folly, the inescapability of passing on one's inheritance is a cause of much despair (2:13-14, 20-22).

---
12. Zimmerli, "Prediger," 129.

When Qohelet realized that a fool is every bit as likely to inherit as the wise, he hated the deeds done under the sun and the work of the worker (2:15–17, 18–19), which explains his fivefold evaluation of the problem of inheritance as הבל (2:15, 17, 19, 21, 23).

The context in which to understand wisdom and folly in this unit is that of work, and specifically working to store up an inheritance. And so the conclusion to this initial observation that wisdom is better than folly is that toil results only in grief and pain, and consists only of burden (2:22–23).

2:24–26

As in 2:21, the royal fiction is no longer important, or at the very least, the idea that a king should better be able to discern a path out of vanity is discarded. Instead Qohelet presents the problem which every person must consider. The conclusion to this first observation panel provides two ways to approach life, which is emphasized by its repetition, as evinced through this structure:

Preface: One can do nothing better than **see** (וראה) satisfaction in their toil (2.24a–b)

    A **I saw** (יתיאר) this was a gift from the hand of God (2:24c)

      B No enjoyment without God (2:25)

    A` God gives to those who please him (2:26a)

      B` Sinners are given the burden, which is vanity (2:26b)

This fourth unit, as noted earlier, acts as a coda to the first panel. Although it is much shorter than the other units, it has a similar structure, with a preface and then an ABA`B` pattern (rather than the ABB`A` pattern we have become attuned to). If wisdom doesn't get him ahead, if pleasure doesn't satisfy, if fools will inherit the fruits of his labor, then Qohelet has nowhere else to go except to fall back on his knowledge of God as creator. These verses have the second and third mentions of God in the book (the first was in 1:13), and he is portrayed here as sovereign beyond the vanity of this world.

PART 2: THE OBSERVATION PANELS

The preface summarizes what Qohelet's investigations have uncovered, that is, to see the good in their work (2:24a–b). The construction גם־זה (also this) has occurred five times so far (1:17; 2:15, 19, 21, 23, 26), always in conjunction with הבל or chasing the wind. But in 2:24 it surprises the reader, as Qohelet instead saw that eating and drinking and seeing the good in their work is a gift of God (2:24). This is reinforced in 2:26a, with God giving, to the one who is "good before him," wisdom, knowledge and joy. The contrast is to the B sections, where Qohelet questions the possibility of eating with joy apart from God (2:25); moreover, should such a person receive an inheritance, even what they have will be taken from them and given to one who is "good before God." This would truly be a vanity and a chasing after wind (2:26b).

The structure of this concluding unit contrasts two ways to work. According to my proposed ABA`B` structure for this final unit, the A sections provide the positive opportunities to find meaning under the sun, for one who receives all things as a gift from the hand of God. The B sections provide the vain alternative, namely trying to enjoy life apart from the creator (2:25). Not only is this a vain pursuit, but one that God actively punishes, with the second half of 2:26 explaining that the one who is separated from God (חוטא, the sinner) will be burdened, with whatever was accrued being confiscated and regifted (cf. Luke 19:11–27, esp. 26).

In essence, the answer is seen in the contrast between gift and task, or, more pleasingly in German, *Gabe und Aufgabe*. Others may want to read this unit (or indeed the entire panel) as summed up by the final clause, "this too is vanity and a chasing after wind," which is entirely logical and provides support for a pessimistic reading of the book. However, reading these verses as drawing out the negative half of the contrast (2:26b) seems to make more sense of the thrust, as well as the rhetorical force of this first of several *carpe diem* statements throughout the book (for similar statements, see 3:13; 5:17; 8:15; 9:7).[13] That is, there is indeed a good

---

13. This important topic, that of the contrast between enjoyment and הבל in Ecclesiastes, is discussed by others. See for instance Lee, *Vitality of Enjoyment*. Perhaps it will suffice for the purposes of this book to suggest that

way to live under the sun, for there is nothing better (אֵין־טוֹב בָּאָדָם, 2:24) than to receive and enjoy the goodness of God's creation as a gift. Or, as Roger Whybray puts it, "<u>God</u> may <u>give</u> joy and pleasure; <u>man</u> can never achieve it for himself, however hard he may try."[14]

Summary of 1:12—2:26

Qohelet makes good use of many first-person verbs to make this first panel a clear description of his observations. Apart from the absence in the first unit of an introductory use of רָאָה, the rest of the panel has a clear and consistent pattern. In each unit the observation proper is introduced with the purpose or a summary of what Qohelet hopes to find, followed by what Qohelet actually saw to be the case. The three observation panels which follow dispense with the preface seen in this first panel, instead launching directly into Qohelet's observations.

This first panel has raised the question of where meaning can be found. Can the king find the answer? Burdensome work would seem to make the answer "no" (1:12–18). Could pleasure and achievement be the answer? The transient nature of it all would seem to make the answer "no" (2:1–11). What of the wisdom of saving for one's descendants? The uncertainty of their character would seem to make the answer "no" (2:12–23).

The only positive answer Qohelet can find is in enjoying work as a gift of God, for no one can find enjoyment without him, and to try to do so—which includes finding meaning in work itself, in building and accumulating, and in accumulating for one's descendants—is vanity and snatching after wind.

This is not all Qohelet will have to say on the matter, but in this first panel he has begun to outline the results of his observations thus far. Enjoyment of God's gifts might not be the ultimate best, but it is a genuine good and strikes a stark contrast with the alternative of vain accumulation with no chance for enjoyment.

Qohelet's more sparse *carpe diem* statements are all the more stark against the repeated instances of vanity observed by Qohelet.

14. Whybray, "Qoheleth, Preacher of Joy," 89. Emphasis original.

PART 2: THE OBSERVATION PANELS

OBSERVATION PANEL 1 (1:12—2:26)		
Unit	Use of ראה at the beginning of a unit	Use of ראה at the end of a unit
1:12–18	ראיתי (1:14)	—
2:1–11	אראה (2:3)	—
2:12–23	ראיתי (2:13)	—
2:24–26	ראיתי (2:24)	—

This panel has served as a good case study as it is clearly separated from the preceding and succeeding material (respectively, the poetic reflections on creation and time) and clearly demonstrates the use of ראה (in general) and ראיתי/אראה (in particular) as a structuring element.

Observation Panel 2 (3:10—4:16)

As noted above, in the first observation panel Qohelet tuned the reader in to the importance of the verb ראה in structuring his observations. That was accentuated through the double usage of the verb in three of the four units. With the first wisdom panel (3:1–9) providing a clear break between the two observation panels, this second observation panel has a structure in which the units do not just begin with the first-person declension of ראה, but the units are, with the exception of the first, bookended with אראה/ראיתי. Furthermore, there is also what I call a "wisdom interlude" (4:5–6), a short ABA` aphorism which falls in between the third and fourth units in order to provide sapiential support to what is stated observationally.

Chapter 3 begins with a poem, which concludes with the rhetorical question in 3:9, מה־יתרון (cf. 1:3; 5:15). The next verse begins with the key verb, ראה, in the *qatal* (3:10), and it occurs four further times in the *qatal* within the panel (3:16, 22; 4:7, 15), as well as twice in the *yiqtol* (4:1, 7). Taken as the outline of this panel, it reveals four units. The first unit stands out as a series of three statements—one observation and two conclusions: ראיתי

(3:10); יְדַעְתִּי (3:12); יְדַעְתִּי (3:14).¹⁵ The following three units, while different to the first, all conform to a similar pattern to each other, providing three clearly delineated structural blocks, each of which are bookended with "I saw." These are 3:16–22; 4:1–4; and 4:7–16. These three are each tightly structured units which follow an internal ABBA structure. The wisdom interlude in 4:5–6 introduces the material following in 4:7–15.¹⁶

> 3:10–15 (רָאִיתִי at 3:10, יְדַעְתִּי at 3:12, 14) I saw beauty in the midst of burdens
>
> 3:16–22 (רָאִיתִי at 3:16, 22) I saw justice in the context of death
>
> 4:1–4 (אֶרְאֶה at 4:1, רָאִיתִי at 4:4) I saw that oppression makes death seem preferable
>
> 4:5–6 Wisdom interlude encouraging the wise path of moderation
>
> 4:7–16 (אֶרְאֶה at 4:7, רָאִיתִי at 4:15) I saw two vanities (workaholism, fame) solved

As with the first observation panel, 3:10—4:16 continues to highlight the existential problem of finding one's meaning in pursuing things which will inevitably fail.

3:10–15

Defining the first unit of this second observation panel is complex, as the multiple approaches to this chapter to show the difficulty of deciding on the structural boundaries. Reinert lists over a dozen commentators, who variously suggest the boundaries of the first unit of chapter 3 could be 3:1–8; 3:1–9; and 3:1–15—or indeed the whole chapter, 3:1–22.¹⁷ The reasons for the difficulty of dividing the chapter up are clear. 3:10–15 has undeniable resonance

---

15. Again, see our discussion earlier regarding Qohelet's use of both these verbs, as noted by Zimmerli, "Prediger," 129.

16. This "wisdom interlude" will be discussed in detail below, along with a similar "observation interlude," which occurs within a wisdom panel.

17. Reinert, *Die Salomofiktion*, 98.

PART 2: THE OBSERVATION PANELS

with what precedes it, with overlapping vocabulary and themes, not least the link between the language for time, with twenty-nine occurrences of עת (time) in 3:1–8, a further one in 3:11, and then also in 3:17 (which repeats the second part of the opening refrain [3:1b] almost word for word). In this sense, 3:10–15 could be described as an observation response to the wisdom poem. Not only this, but 3:10–15 continues to think "big picture," describing the things which are done in the context of עלם/עולם (age/eternity, 3:11, 14), a broader understanding of time than either זמן (season, 3:1a) or עת (3:1b–8), which puts all these activities into perspective. But, as well as linking to the passage immediately preceding it (not to mention the perspective introduced with the opening poem), 3:10–15 also points forward, providing the appropriate context to what will be a confronting panel to follow: life has many burdens, but nonetheless there is beauty and much to be enjoyed at the hand of God. Therefore, although we would not be incorrect to note this as a hinge passage, these are Qohelet's observations, signaled by the use of ראיתי, and hence it is best to view these verses as the first unit of a new observation panel. As both a summary of what precedes, but also looking forward, this unit introduces the observation panel with three short sections:

> A **I saw** (ראיתי) that life is burdensome, yet God provides beauty (3:10–11)
>
> B I understood (ידעתי) that God has given enjoyment in life as a gift (3:12–13)
>
> B` I understood (ידעתי) that God's works alone are eternal (3:14–15)

This unit is clearly structured around the three first-person *qatal* verbs beginning each section, providing first observation (3:10–11) and then analysis (3:12–13, 14–15). As with 1:12–18, the observations of ראיתי are coupled with the dual conclusions of ידעתי to form the three parts of this unit with an ABB` structure. There are multiple points of connection between the three parts, not least being each part beginning with a first-person *qatal* verb. Building on the concluding unit to the previous observation panel, in each section the works and sovereignty of God are highlighted.

3:11 describes everything God has done (את־הכל עשה) and the deeds which God has done (את־המעשה אשר־עשה האלהים). 3:12 talks about what people are able to do (ולעשות), while 3:14 twice describes God's deeds, again with עשה. Vocabulary pertaining to work is found in each section, with עשה six times (3:11 [x3], 12, 14 [x2]), as well as ענה (3:10) and עמל (3:13).

There is also a theme throughout these six verses of God as the giver, with נתן אלהים in 3:10, מתת אלהים in 3:13, and apophatically in 3:14, where no one is able to add or take from what God has done (אין להוסיף וממנו אין לגרע).

Following on from the wisdom poem on time, this unit explains what can be known in a world of uncertainty and ignorance. Despite the overwhelming context of eternity and the abject finitude of humanity, God's works alone remain into eternity, and God remains the only source of good gifts, including here the real possibility of enjoyment and satisfaction.

3:16–22

This second unit is introduced as a continuation of the thrust of the previous unit, with a further observation of Qohelet: ועוד ראיתי (again/further I saw). As with the first unit of this panel, the sections are marked out by four first-person *qatal* verbs, with ראיתי beginning and ending the unit (3:16, 22) and the central sections describing Qohelet's self-talk: אמרתי אני בלבי (3:17, 18). This unit has an ABB`A` structure.

    A **I saw** (ראיתי) under the sun there is wickedness (3:16)

        B I said (אמרתי) God will judge (3:17)

        B' I said (אמרתי) God will test (3:18–21)

    A' **I saw** (וראיתי) there is nothing better than to enjoy life (3:22)

Both A sections describe the activities of human beings. 3:16 describes the failures of people to adjudicate justly, with righteousness and wickedness being confused. The conclusion in 3:22 describes all that people can do, namely, doing their best to enjoy life in a world that has become corrupted and where ignorance reigns, where despite no one being able to bring about justice, so too is no one able to bring about knowledge of the future (כי מי יביאנו לראות במה שיהיה אחריו).

The B sections compare two groups. In 3:17 people are divided into two categories: הצדיק and הרשע (righteous and wicked), while in 3:18–21 all creation is divided into two categories: האדם and הבהמה (human and animal). It is the lack of distinction between these two groups which frustrates Qohelet's investigations. There should be an easy way to distinguish between the righteous and the wicked, and he tells himself (אמרתי אני בלבי) that despite people's inability in this regard (3:16) that God is able (3:17). Nonetheless, from the vantage point of being under the sun, such discernment is lacking, as human and beast alike die, and Qohelet has no special revelation regarding the destination of their spirits.

The result is that the project of pursuing justice (3:16–22), while admirable, is not the place to find meaning. This must be the case, because people generally die with unfulfilled pursuits, or, in a similar vein, if one's life is set on vengeance, the object of one's vengeance may well die, leaving the evildoer unpunished and the avenger unavenged. People under the sun are not in a position to know what will happen to them, and if the pursuit of justice is supposed to give meaning, in its place will be found only vanity.

4:1–4

4:1–4 begins and ends with what Qohelet observes as the problem of oppression, namely the misuse of power and jealousy as the driving motivations for all achievement. In this short section Qohelet draws out one extreme of the tension of living under the sun. While there may well be much good in life, simply being alive means experiencing oppression. Picking up on the theme of death from the previous section, if oppression is the reality and tears will remain uncomforted, then death—or, even better, non-existence—is floated as a very realistic solution, especially as Qohelet's readers now understand that their efforts to change things will always leave them unfulfilled.

A **I saw** (וארא) works of oppression under the sun (4:1)
   B Death is preferable to living under oppression (4:2)
   B` Non-existence is preferable to having seen the evil under the sun (4:3)
A` **I saw** (וראיתי) achievement stems only from jealousy and is vanity (4:4)

This short ABB`A` unit divides by verses, with the first and last featuring ראיתי/אראה. Both 4:1 and 4:4 contain a redundant/emphatic אני: 4:1 "Then I turned—I—and I saw all the ...," 4:4: "I saw—I—all the ..." This similar formula is seen with את־כל (2x in 4:4), and then patterns of four: in 4:1 there is a fourfold use of עשק (to oppress), which occurs four times as a participle, albeit in different forms each time, while in 4:4 the pattern of four is made up of four near-synonyms for work, with עמל, כשרון, מעשה and then, for the fourth, what Qohelet describes as work's functional equivalent, namely כי הוא קנאת־איש מרעהו (for this is one's envy over their friend).

The B sections both contain rather depressing comparisons and some interesting Hebrew constructions. 4:2 begins with *waw*-infinitive-אני, which Qohelet uses in place of a first-person *qatal*, and he then compares death favorably with life.[18] 4:3 begins with one of Qohelet's many uses of the טוב ... מן construction, comparing nonexistence favorably to ever having lived. There is an inbuilt redundancy in both comparisons, as in 4:2 the dead are called את־המתים ש ... מתו and the living are similarly called החיים אשר חיים .... Meanwhile, in 4:3 the experiences which the non-existent people missed out on are detailed, as Qohelet explains they fortunately did not have to observe the evil done under the sun.

---

18. On this construction see Waltke and O'Connor, *Introduction to Biblical Hebrew Syntax*, 597, who call this the "systematic exception" to the regular use of the infinitive absolute.

PART 2: THE OBSERVATION PANELS

In this unit Qohelet is close to his rhetorically darkest point (although cf. 6:3). His observations have not provided much hope, as oppression is the norm and all work is tainted by jealousy. Although elsewhere he sees light, at this point there is only darkness.

4:5–6

An interesting feature of this panel is the two-verse wisdom saying in 4:5–6.[19] This ties the whole section together as it discusses the extremes of complete inaction and overaction, but also presents a middle ground against the extremes of 4:5 and 4:6b, that of quiet contentment as something that is "better" (4:6a). Furthermore, this wisdom saying follows an ABA` structure, similar to that seen in the rest of the observation sections:

A The lazy fool has nothing (4:5)

4:5 הכסיל חבק את־ידיו ואכל את־בשרו:

B The wise has enough (4:6a)

4:6a טוב מלא כף נחת

A` The workaholic fool has only vanity (4:6b)

4:6b ממלא חפנים עמל ורעות רוח:

Although these three clauses could be construed as two separate sayings (4:5 and 4:6), it seems prudent to read them together as describing three possibilities of being. Person 1 (4:5) is a fool. They do nothing—they fold their hands. Qohelet is perhaps adapting Proverbs 6:10//24:33 as the sluggard is described as clasping their hands to rest (חבק ידים לשכב). In the flow of the panel it is possible that this person has become so overwhelmed by the oppression and jealousy observed under the sun that they no longer have confidence in the goodness of work. But because they do not work, they cannot eat. The only thing they have to hand is their own flesh (ואכל את־בשרו). Person 3, on the other extreme (4:6b), works much. Both their hands are occupied with labor, and while they

---

19. As mentioned above, this "wisdom interlude" will be dealt with in more detail below.

have full hands, there is no meaning; they are chasing the wind. Person 2 (4:6a), however, is wise. Only one of their hands is mentioned, which is full of rest. This is like the fool, except that is only half of their story. The other half of the story is to be filled in by the reader, which is that their other hand is occupied with labor. This person understands their own limits and is able to work as well as rest, with the key being that they are not searching for meaning in their labor or in their rest.

There are two or perhaps three instances of gapping or ellipsis in this short aphorism. הכסיל is identified in 4:5, but there is no corresponding explicit mention of the wise person. Similarly, the content of the wise person's other hand is not mentioned and must be supplied by the reader. Furthermore, person 3 is not identified—they would seem to be a fool, but perhaps the word הכסיל is not precise enough, as they do not fit the typical depiction of a profligate fool. Nonetheless, the parallelism works, and if the shoe fits, the workaholic must wear it—they are indeed a fool. This verse introduces the טוב ... מן pattern, which will be used in the unit following (4:9, 13), but it also flags the theme of the problem of workaholism and equates it to folly (cf. 4:7-12). Although occurring within an observation panel, instead of an observation signaled by ראה, Qohelet inserts this aphorism in between two observation units to achieve much the same end.

4:7-16

At first glance these verses, taken together, do not constitute one unit. It is clear they tell two different stories and the logical connection is not immediately evident. However, noting the use of אראה in 4:7 and ראיתי in 4:15, multiple points of correspondence within this unit become clear. Parallel negative observations at the beginning and end of the unit (4:7-8, 15-16) frame parallel positive exhortations in the center (4:9-12, 13), revealing yet another ABB`A` structure. While there are two distinct stories or observations, each of which can be understood without reference to the other, they together form one cohesive unit.

PART 2: THE OBSERVATION PANELS

  A **I saw** (וראה) the vanity of life without friends (4:7–8)

    B Arranging your life so you have friends is better (4:9–12)

    B` Staying poor and wise rather than famous and foolish is better (4:13–14)

  A` **I saw** (ראיתי) the vanity of placing hope in leaders under the sun (4:15–16)

The first half expands on the wisdom interlude (4:5–6): the workaholic might have much, except they are missing out on the life which, in the context of vanity, is so often extolled as a good thing. Here in 4:7–8 the rich workaholic misses out on friends, who, as 4:9–12 explains, are invaluable. This explains what it is they have both hands full of in 4:6b, namely, work and its fruits, whereas the wise person has one handful of meaningful labor, with the other free to embrace the gifts of rest and friendship.

Structurally, parallels between the A sections are evident, as they describe again what Qohelet has seen under the sun. In 4:7 Qohelet sees vanity under the sun, while in 4:15 he sees people going about under the sun. Both A sections describe groups of people. In the first there is a lack: one without a second, not even a son or a brother (4:8). In 4:15 only a second is described, who is the successor to a first. 4:16 goes on to talk about people, people who are אין־קץ (without end). This same formula, ... אין־קץ לכל, is used in the first A section also. While in 4:16 it refers to the endless supply of people, in 4:8 it describes the frustration of the rich person, for whom there is no end to all the riches. These never-ceasing flows of money and riches observed by Qohelet are a sign that there is a problem inherent in both these situations.

The two central B sections are signaled with the טוב ... מן (better than) comparisons in 4:9 and 4:13, as foreshadowed by the use of this structure in the second verse of the wisdom interlude (4:6). They both contrast one good option with another very common occurrence. In the first instance the good is to work with a friend rather than to work alone, and in the second the good is the one who is young, poor and wise rather than a king who is old and a fool. Both of these comparisons are explained further, with two better than one justified with three theoreticals, introduced as they are with כי אם (4:10), גם־אם (4:11) and ואם (4:12). The second B section has a similar further explanation, with the one who is young, poor and wise described twice in clauses beginning first with כי and then with כי גם (4:14).

This unit draws together two observations. The first is that workaholism is a dead end, regardless of the wealth accrued. The second observes a mass of people following a leader who will soon be forgotten, like all those who went beforehand. In both instances Qohelet can justify a better path: In the first it is to have a friend to work alongside, as the benefits are great. In the second it means choosing wisdom over folly, regardless of one's provenance, as a rich king may well be a fool, but far better is to have someone who, though young and poor, has wisdom.

Summary of 3:10—4:16

This second observation panel has provided a challenging mix of observations and conclusions. There are limits to human possibility in the midst of injustice and there are depraved motives behind much of human achievement, but nonetheless there is wisdom in moderation and in working with a friend. And despite shortcomings of wisdom, there remain some successes.

The verb ראיתי/אראה has provided the structure to the units within the panels, with some fairly clear pointers to the sections within them. The boundaries between the units are not completely impermeable, as is seen especially with the close links between the wisdom poem (3:1–9) and the first unit (3:10–15), but also with the application of the concepts in the wisdom interlude (4:5–6) to the discussion in the first half of the final unit (4:7–12). But this does not negate the multiple points of correspondence within each of the units, which hold them together structurally and conceptually.

PART 2: THE OBSERVATION PANELS

OBSERVATION PANEL 2 (3:10—4:16)		
Unit	Use of ראה at the beginning of a unit	Use of ראה at the end of a unit
3:10–15	ראיתי (3:10)	—
3:16–22	ראיתי (3:16)	ראיתי (3:22)
4:1–4	אראה (4:1)	ראיתי (4:4)
4:7–16	אראה (4:7)	ראיתי (4:15)

Observation Panel 3 (5:12[13]—6:12)[20]

Following the second observation section (3:10—4:16), there are no further first-person occurrences of the verb ראה until 5:12[13], which is the first of a group of three occurrences in relatively close succession: 5:12[13], 17[18]; and 6:1.[21] Looking closely at what follows, each occurrence begins a unit with a structure not dissimilar to the previous block of first-person observation, with each individual section having a similar AB(B`)A` concentric structure.

5:12–16 I saw an evil sickness (ראיתי at 5:12)

5:12 יש רעה חולה ראיתי תחת השמש [. . .]:

5:17–19 I saw the good gift (ראיתי at 5:17)

5:17 הנה אשר־ראיתי אני טוב [. . .]:

6:1–12 I saw another evil (ראיתי at 6:1)

6:1 יש רעה אשר ראיתי תחת השמש [. . .]:

---

20. The Hebrew verse ordering of chapter 4 continues to verse 17, meaning that the English text of chapter 5 is one verse out of sync.

21. There is one second-person occurrence of ראה at 5:7[8], forming part of a rhetorical exhortation or wisdom "instruction". Longman, *Book of Ecclesiastes*, 156. It is also worth mentioning that there are no first-person verbs at all in the intervening period, 4:17—5:11.

5:12–16[13–17]

5:12 begins with Qohelet describing what he has observed: he has seen (ראיתי) an evil sickness (רעה חולה) under the sun. This phrase is repeated in his conclusion to this unit (5:15–16), as he again mentions רעה חולה in 5:15, and simply חולה in 5:16. The story in between is that of the cruel master: wealth. And life too mimics this: nakedness at the beginning and end, with toil first accruing, then diminishing one's wealth (5:14). The whole existence of one suffering under this sickness is described as "eating in darkness," pointing to the degradation of what should be a good thing.[22] This has parallels with the previous observation panel, where the workaholic pauses to ask why they work as they do for no relational or joyous gain (esp. 4:8). The parallels between the opening and closing reveal this section to have an ABA` structure:

A There is an evil sickness (רעה חולה) regarding wealth that **I saw** (ראיתי) under the sun (5:12–13)

B You go as you came: with nothing (5:14)

A` There is an evil sickness (רעה חולה) about coming and going in darkness (5:15–16)

This opening unit discusses רעה חולה. The phrase occurs in 5:12 and 5:15, with רעה occurring a second time in 5:12 and חולה occurring a further time in 5:16. In both A sections there is a discussion about the purpose of acquiring, when wealth (עשר) is wicked (רעה) (5:12) and is easily expunged (5:13). Therefore 5:15 again asks the question, מה-יתרון, as trying to find meaning by acquiring wealth is akin to laboring after wind. Returning to the image of the workaholic from 4:8, Qohelet describes someone whose only reward is to eat alone in the dark (5:16).

At the center of this unit (5:14) is the description of the person with no net gain, taking nothing with them (מאומה, cf. 5:13). This net zero result is in stark contrast to the busyness implied by

---

22. See especially the positive uses of אכל in the verses following (5:18–19), as well as the two occurrences in 6:2, describing again what is being missed out on: the joy of eating of the fruits of their labor.

the many verbs of action in this verse, with נשא, בוא, שוב, יצא and הלך.

5:17–19[18–20]

The panel began with a negative unit in 5:12–16 and will end with a negative in 6:1–12, but in this central unit Qohelet emphasizes the positive. The interjection הנה (Look!) begins this section, and here Qohelet describes what he sees (ראיתי) to be good (5:17a). He explains it is good for people to find enjoyment (literally, "to see goodness," לראת טובה) in their work during their few days under the sun (5:17). The conclusion in 5:19 focuses on the joy (שמחה) which God gives to people. These things are described in 5:17 as given (נתן) by God; likewise, in 5:18 all things are given by God (נתן), and are a gift of God (מתת). This links back to Qohelet's core understanding of God as sovereign, and in this case the way to understand what is good in the midst of the short life of a human (1:4) is to acknowledge God as the giver and enjoy his gifts.

As Bartholomew notes, there is some discussion over the root ענה in 5:19, which has a negative meaning in 1:13 and 3:10 (to keep busy/be occupied with), but here could well be the more neutral or even positive "to answer, to give back."[23] That is, rather than the worries of 6:3, where that person is unable to enjoy the fruit of their toil, in 5:19 God gives them over to truly enjoy what they have received (cf. 2:24–26). The more common translation of ענה here as "keep occupied" implies a somewhat perverse divinely granted amnesia which makes little sense of the thrust of these verses. The more optimistic reading I have adopted makes more sense of this unit's central position in the panel, as well as the immediate context of good things given as a good gift by a good God.

    A Look!—**I saw** (ראיתי) good under the sun (5:17)
        B The enjoyment of wealth is a gift of God (5:18)
    A' God gives people joy (5:19)

---

23. Bartholomew, *Ecclesiastes*, 227, in conversation with N. Lohfink.

This short ABA' unit contrasts with the units either side, as it is replete with positive imagery, instead of the evil sicknesses Qohelet has seen there. It begins by pointing out what Qohelet has seen, drawing attention to what he has seen (ראיתי) with הנה. Twice in 5:17 Qohelet says it is possible to see good, seeing יפה (beauty/fittingness) and the opportunity to eat and drink without the negative connotations of a verse earlier. In both 5:17 and 5:19 the sphere of one's enjoyment is חיי (life), and it is there that God will answer people with שמחה (5:19).

In the central B section the focus is twice on what God gives, which includes the good things of עשר (riches), נכסים (wealth), the ability to eat, to take up their portion (לשאת את־חלקו), and to find joy (שמחה) in their labor (5:18).

6:1–12

This third unit returns to the theme of the first unit, which is especially evident when comparing the first verses of the respective units:

6:1 יש רעה אשר <u>ראיתי</u> תחת השמש

5:12 יש רעה חולה <u>ראיתי</u> תחת השמש

As with the first unit, this presents the negative foil for the central optimistic section, and does so with an ABB'A' pattern:

A **I saw** (ראיתי) the evil (רעה) of wealth under the sun when God is sovereign (6:1–2)

   B Having much does not satisfy (6:3–6)

   B' People are not able to be satisfied (6:7–11)

A' The ignorance about people under the sun (6:12)

The first A section (6:1–2) begins by talking about רעה (6:1) and concludes with the fuller formulation, וחלי רע הוא (6:2). It describes what God has given, namely עשר, but also that God does not necessarily give people the opportunity to enjoy said wealth.

PART 2: THE OBSERVATION PANELS

This reiterates the conclusion after the first set of observations in 2:24–26. The second A section continues this thought, in light of God's sovereignty over giving and taking, that people are insignificant and ignorant. The verse also holds together with some pleasing assonance in the early stages of the three stichs, with כי מי־יגיד and ימי־חיי, מי.

The B sections take up two examples to illustrate this point, first from 6:3–6, with the observation that having much, whether wealth or descendants, is no guarantee of enjoyment, of respect in death, or of one's destination after death. Large numbers hold this section together, as the word רב occurs twice in 6:3, alongside one hundred (6:3) and one thousand (6:6), in reference to numbers of years and descendants. Qohelet's considered decision (אמרתי) is, if there is no enjoyment, that one who is stillborn is better off (6:3).

The second B section similarly has a טוב . . . מן comparison, although in this instance it concerns being satisfied with what one has rather than striving for more. Twice in this section comes the question מה־יותר/מה־יתר (6:8, 11; cf. 1:3; 5:15). As with 6:3, the question of רב (many) is repeated, although in this instance the result is more explicit: כי יש דברים הרבה מרבים הבל (when there are a multiplicity of words, vanity is multiplied, 6:11). Along with these links there is also the double use of נפש (soul, 6:7, 9; cf. 6:3) and the fortunes of אדם (person), which dominates the second half of this unit (6:7, 10, 11, 12 [x2]).

Summary of 5:12—6:12

The three units of this third panel are distinct from the other observation panels because of the way in which together they tell a story. There is overlapping vocabulary across the three units as well as tensions drawn out between them, as what may be vanity in one context is a good in another. Similarly, where God is observed as a giver of good things, so too is he depicted as callous, giving the good yet not providing the necessary capability to enjoy that good. That the units work together as one larger ABA` structure is evident from the use of ראיתי to begin each unit, the reuse of רעה

59

חולה in the first and third units, and the common themes running through each of them. What is less clear is the way the resulting structure is to be interpreted. My approach is to read the B unit (5:17–19) as the honey in the sandwich, the good to be enjoyed, despite the overwhelming negative experience either side. Others taking the pessimistic reading will of course read the A units (5:12–16; 6:1–12) as Qohelet's conclusion, with the optimistic hope in the center comprehensively disproved by the experiences and observations either side of them, with the center serving only to further heighten the depths of his pessimism.

OBSERVATION PANEL 3 (5:12—6:12)		
Unit	Use of ראה at the beginning of a unit	Use of ראה at the end of a unit
5:12–16	ראיתי (5:12)	—
5:17–19	ראיתי (5:17)	—
6:1–12	ראיתי (6:1)	—

Observation Panel 4 (7:15—9:13)

The longest of the first-person observation panels, this fourth panel (7:15—9:13) resumes the observations at 7:15 with Qohelet's first ראיתי since 6:1. It occurs five times in total in this panel (7:15; 8:9, 10, 17; 9:13), although, as with the first observation panel, this too draws on other conjugations of the verb ראה for discerning its structure. This distinguishes it from the second and third panels, which make use only of the first-person verb, however this panel is consistent with the second in having every unit bookended by the verb. It is clearly delineated from the wisdom collection which follows it, with a complete absence of any conjugations of the verb ראה until the double (and final) occurrence of ראיתי in the observation interlude at 10:5–7.[24] On first appraisal, the beginning point of the panel is complicated by the fact that ראה occurs three times immediately prior to ראיתי at 7:15 (in 7:11, 13, 14). However,

---

24. See below on Wisdom Collection 4.

PART 2: THE OBSERVATION PANELS

these occurrences are not Qohelet's observations, but wisdom exhortations which belong to the preceding wisdom panel (7:1–14). Furthermore, the first-person use of ראה has been the consistent marker of the beginning of a new observation section throughout the book (cf. 1:14; 3:10; 5:12); other variants of ראה have played a supporting role.

> 7:15–28a (ראיתי at 7:15, ראה at 7:27) I've seen it all, and I did not find righteousness or wisdom
>
> 7:28b—8:9 (ראה at 7:29, ראיתי at 8:9) I saw that God made people upright; they pursued many schemes
>
> 8:10–16 (ראיתי at 8:10, לראות at 8:16) I saw a world where the fates of the wicked and the righteous are the same
>
> 8:17—9:10 (ראיתי at 8:17, ראה at 9:9) I saw how hard it is for people to understand God
>
> 9:11–13 (ראה at 9:11, ראיתי at 9:13) I saw there is wisdom in understanding the limits of human perception

This final observation panel is by far the longest of the observation panels at forty-five verses.[25] Furthermore, by this stage of the book, not only does Qohelet have more observations, but they also seem to tend toward the wisdom genre exemplified in the wisdom panels. Despite this, the "seeing" vocabulary (ראה and its declensions) permeates this panel much more thoroughly than our previous observation panel (5:12—6:12). This thoroughgoing use of ראה is a cue to the reader, despite the heightened sapiential character, that they are still being taught through Qohelet's observations rather than through a wisdom collection.

7:15–28a

This first unit is bookended with discoveries: "I have seen everything in my vain life" (7:15); "Look at what I have found" (7:27).

---

25. For reference, the observation panels are, in order, thirty-three, twenty-nine, twenty, and forty-five verses long.

It forms another ABB`A` structure, and ראה is used first as ראיתי (7:15) and then as an imperative in combination with מצאתי (I found, 7:27).

    A **I saw** (ראיתי) the confusion of fates of the righteous and the wicked (7:15)
        B You can't be righteous (7:16–22)
        B` You can't be wise (7:23–26)
    A` **Look** (ראה): I found that I couldn't find wisdom (7:27–28a)

This final panel begins with a unit describing a negative: Qohelet talks about all the things he could not find out. It begins and ends with what Qohelet has observed, and in both cases he found nothing. What the hopeful reader of Proverbs would expect, namely, the prospering of the righteous and the withering of the wicked, is reversed. This is explained through a double use of צדיק (righteousness) combined with the couplet of רשע and רעה (wicked/evil, 7:15). In the conclusion Qohelet is similarly frustrated, as he says, "look at what I have found ... I couldn't find" (7:27–28a). In the A sections Qohelet has drawn attention to what he has not found: he has not seen the rewards of morality, nor has he been able to find what he sought.

These failures frame two sections (7:16–22, 23–26) which deal with the two topics Qohelet has sought an answer to. The first B section (7:16–22), while continuing the theme of righteousness (twice in 7:15), begins with four jussive clauses and two questions with the repeated pattern of אל־ ... ואל־ ... למה (7:16–17). In light of what he has seen in 7:15, Qohelet bids his listeners to not be overly concerned with the sole pursuit of righteousness (אל־תהי צדיק הרבה, 7:16), as well as reminding them that there is no one on earth who will be righteous (אדם אין צדיק בארץ, 7:20); trying to find meaning in legalistic perfectionism, especially in light of the distortion of the concept of retribution (7:15), will result only in more vanity.

In the second B section (7:23–26), Qohelet similarly counsels against the single-minded pursuit of what should be another good. In the first it was righteousness, in the second it is wisdom. He tested this by wisdom (7:23a); he said "Let me be wise" (7:23b); he turned to seek out wisdom (7:25). As with the first B section, here too we find another pair of questions in 7:24 as well as the use of repetition as a superlative: רָחוֹק מַה־שֶּׁהָיָה וְעָמֹק עָמֹק מִי יִמְצָאֶנּוּ.[26] But the far off and the very deep things of God, especially against the foil of Lady Folly (7:26), were unattainable for Qohelet. Continuing the language of מצא (7:24, 26), the second B section thus leads into the final A section with its threefold use of מצא.

7:28b—8:9

The beginning of this unit is hard to pin down. The imperative ראה at the beginning of 7:27 gives the earliest point for the end of the first unit, while ראה in 7:29, also an imperative, provides the first unit's *terminus ad quem*. The אשר which begins 7:28 gives further information to the content of 7:27, so it seems appropriate to continue until at least the middle of that verse. The number אחד (one) in 7:27 and 7:28b naturally seem to link these verses together, but אדם in 7:28b (twice) and 8:1 appears to join those two verses together also. The same could be said for מצא in 7:27 (twice), 7:28 (thrice) and 7:29 (once). Given all this, it seems best to follow the lead of Bartholomew, who first addresses the material leading up to and including 7:28a, and then looks at 7:28b separately.[27] This is also apparent in the new sentence begun there in most English translations, which picks up on the lack of a connecting particle (we might expect a *waw*) between מצאתי with the *atnach* locating the midpoint of the verse and the end of that thought, and אדם which follows it and begins the new unit: 7:28b—8:9.

The use of אדם (person/people) which begins this unit is pervasive throughout, occurring in each section: 7:28b, 29; 8:1, 6, 9, showing the focus hinges on people and what can be said about their place under the sun. As with the first, this unit also has an ABB`A` structure:

---

26. Waltke and O'Connor, *Introduction to Biblical Hebrew Syntax*, 233, describe this as the emphatic use of repetitive apposition.

27. Bartholomew, *Ecclesiastes*, 266.

A **Look** (ראה) at what I found: the contrast between people and the God who made them (7:28b–29)
    B The way for people to survive the king (8:1–5a)
    B` People knowing the right time under the king (8:5b–8)
A` **I saw** (ראיתי) people opposing each other (8:9)

The unit continues where the first left off, namely, by talking about what Qohelet is able to find. However, where he was unable to find wisdom in the first unit, he describes what he was able to find with the first A section through an aba` structure based around מצאתי (7:28b–29):

a אדם אחד מאלף <u>מצאתי</u>
b ואשה בכל־אלה <u>לא מצאתי</u>:
a` לבד <u>ראה</u>־זה <u>מצאתי</u>
אשר עשה האלהים את־האדם ישר
והמה בקשו חשבנות רבים:

Expressing the sense of this verse, Qohelet was maybe able to find one person in a thousand, yet a woman, that is, Lady Wisdom,[28] he could not find. And yet, "Look (ראה)! at this that I have found!" This continues with another contrast and the reuse of אדם from 7:28b in 7:29 as well as by its omission in the final clause of 7:29: "yet they (that is, אדם, from 7:29b) sought out many schemes."

The A sections both describe what Qohelet has seen, in both places by means of the added focus of זה (this). In both sections the focus is on deeds: in 7:29 he looks at the people God has made (עשה) while in 8:9 he looks at all that the deeds which are done under the sun (לכל־מעשה אשר נעשה).

The B sections share the use of ידע, with two each (8:1, 5a, 5b, 7), while the first also has four uses of דבר (matter/word) and is bookended with שמר (to keep), first as the imperative שמור (8:2), and then, perhaps as an implied imperative, but formally as the

---

28. Bartholomew, *Ecclesiastes*, 267.

participle, שׁוֹמֵר (8:5). The focus is on using wisdom to survive the rule of a sub-optimal king.

The second B section builds on this to discuss the wisdom that applies itself to appreciating the appropriate time, as עֵת occurs in 8:5b, 6, as well as in the conclusion (8:9). There is a fourfold chain of explanatory כִּי, as Qohelet explains how this should work (8:6a, 6b, 7a, 7b). But although such wisdom would be invaluable, the note of ignorance continues throughout, especially in the final verse of this section with a second fourfold chain: אֵין . . . וְאֵין . . . וְאֵין . . . וְלֹא (isn't, 8:8).

This unit further describes what Qohelet hopes to find but is not able to—wisdom enacted by people. Unfortunately wisdom seems to be more about surviving rather than thriving, as appreciating the time (cf. 3:1–9) does not add to it the requisite benefits it should. Hence the concluding observation, that when people do appreciate the time, they use it to oppress one another (cf. 4:1–4).

8.10–16

This third unit deviates from the established structure a little, so that rather than an ABB`A` structure, an ABA`B` structure is apparent instead, as the topics alternate between on the one hand the disturbing reality observed, and on the other Qohelet's orthodox understanding of how things should be:

> A **I saw** (רָאִיתִי) a confused world, where things went well for the wicked (8:10–12a)
>> B I know how things should be when one fears God (8:12b–13)
>
> A` I said that such a confused state of affairs is vanity (8:14)
>> B` I commended enjoyment even as I continued to try to understand and **to observe** (לִרְאוֹת) wisdom and work (8:15–16)

The beginning of this unit is clear from the presence of רָאִיתִי in 8:9 to close the previous unit, while the next occurrence of רָאִיתִי immediately in the next verse (8:10) signals the beginning of a new unit. The end is less clear, as a majority of translations read 8:16–17a as one continuing sentence at the beginning a new unit (among the few exceptions are the NLT and the *Lutherbibel*). There are good reasons for reading the verses this way, although there are also good reasons for beginning a new section at 8:17 and linking 8:16 to what precedes it. For instance, the story told in 8:15–16 is reminiscent of the contrast seen in 2:24–26, namely, the vivid contrasting of, on the one hand, the life enjoyed from the hand of God with, on the other, the vanity and sleeplessness of the alternative (cf. 4:8; 5:12). That 8:15 and 8:16 are to be understood as part of the one thought is further underscored by 8:16 beginning with כאשר, the "most common temporal conjunction in Hebrew."[29] Therefore, following the structure suggested in this book, it makes sense to read this as anaphoric and concluding the unit, with the next observation unit beginning at 8:17. That said, because this unit contains some of the most difficult verses in all Ecclesiastes,[30] the internal divisions of this unit will always be tendentious and it is understandable why others will reject this division. However, following our outline, which has ראה beginning and ending sections across this fourth observation panel, and for the reasons discussed above, this division is easily possible.

This unit begins with Qohelet describing another thing which he has observed: Qohelet says he saw (ראיתי) two things that do not belong together: רשעים and קדוש מקום. The wicked praise themselves[31] as they go in and out of the holy place, and any punishment against their wickedness has been criminally slow in coming. Indeed, such a delay means they make it to the end of their long life unreprimanded and, worst of all, along the way have influenced others to pursue evil.

Such things are הבל, which is brought up again as bookends to the second A section, as the first and final words of 8:14. There too the good and evil are contrasted, as יש צדיקים who receive the

---

29. Waltke and O'Connor, *Introduction to Biblical Hebrew Syntax*, 203.

30. Longman, *Book of Ecclesiastes*, 219.

31. Reading שכח as שבח with the LXX, as well as taking the reflexive sense of the *hithpael* stem.

treatment more fitting to the evil, while יש רשעים who receive the treatment fitting to the wicked. Again the first-person verb returns here: אמרתי שגם־זה הבל.

And yet, despite the confusion evident in the world, Qohelet wants to hold on to how things should be. As with 3:10–15, the verb ידע is employed to give Qohelet's response. As Ogden explains, כי גם is an adversative, "however" (cf. 4:14; 8:16), for he will not be satisfied with the previous observations having the last word on good and evil.[32] Using ירא three times in 8:12b–13, he affirms that things will go well for those who fear God, and that it will not go well for those who do not fear him, that their lives will not be extended (despite his observations a verse earlier).[33]

Because of this conviction, the second B section goes on to explain how to live in light of this, with another first-person verb commending the enjoyment of the goodness that is to be received at the hand of God. Qohelet commending enjoyment for others (ושבחתי, 8:15) contrasts with the wicked in 8:10 who are commending themselves (*וישתבחו).[34] There is nothing better for people under the sun (אדם תחת השמש) than to enjoy what has been given them by God under the sun (האלהים תחת השמש). The verb ראה returns in 8:16 to draw the section to a conclusion, used as an infinitive along with ידע to explain that his pursuit is not yet over. Qohelet still wants to understand חכמה (wisdom) and he still needs to observe את־הענין (labor), because this task still keeps him up at night, as he explains that his eyes, neither day or night, see any sleep.

The distance between how things are in the A sections and the way things should be in the B sections explain how this unit fits together. And although Qohelet still has much investigation to come and understanding to follow, he shows he is still committed to the reality of God as judge and the enjoyment of gifts from his hand.

32. Ogden, *Qoheleth*, 137.
33. Cf. Isa 38:8.
34. As above, following the LXX rather than the MT.

SEEING WHAT QOHELET SAW

8:17—9:10

This penultimate unit again grapples with the gap between what is observed and what should be the case. As discussed above, לראות at 8:16 signaled the end of the previous unit; וראיתי at 8:17 begins the new unit of observation. This unit has the feeling not of specific observations but of an overarching observation of the reality of life under the sun, which is underscored by the fivefold use of תחת־השמש (8:17; 9:3, 6 and twice in 9:9). This ABB`A` unit first introduces the topic of discussion, then the negative observation balanced by the orthodox hope, with a *carpe diem* section to close.

   A **I saw** (וראיתי) the gap between what God does and what people are able to find out (8:17)

      B I set my heart to explain the lack of difference between the respective fates of the good and evil (9:1–3)

      B` Yet I maintain that life is better than death (9:4–6)

   A` I want people **to see** (ראה) goodness in their lives while they live (9:7–10)

וראיתי introduces this section (8:17) as being about the pursuit for understanding, which is presented in the following fashion:

a ראיתי את־כל־מעשה האלהים
b כי לא יוכל האדם למצוא
c את־המעשה אשר נעשה תחת־השמש
d בשל אשר יעמל האדם לבקש ולא ימצא
e וגם אם־יאמר החכם לדעת לא יוכל למצא:

8:17a and c both describe the work (מעשה) done (נעשה) by God, while 17b, d and e describe the inability of people (האדם) to uncover the meaning behind it, with לא and מצא occurring in each stich, while the role of יוכל in 17b and e is played in 17d by בקש.

The first B section (9:1–3) explains that the reason God's work is so difficult to understand is because of Qohelet's oft-repeated problem with the righteous and the wicked being undifferentiated even at the point of death. There is a confluence of vocabulary around this topic of morality, with רשע, צדיק, הצדיקים, טוב (2x), טהור, טמא, זבח (people who do and don't offer sacrifices), שבע (people who do and don't take oaths), מלא רע, רע, and finally הוללות, all packed into these three verses. Qohelet's concern is that God is not making an objective distinction between people based on their behavior, and that all of these shall die without distinction.

Ogden describes the כי beginning the next section (9:4–6) as an asseverative, which breaks what follows from what precedes and puts the attention on the מי.[35] Qohelet's conviction is that whoever is alive can appreciate what is good, which is as different to those who are dead as is a living dog to a dead lion. Appropriately חי (life) appears three times in 9:4–5 (as it also does in 9:9), which shows how this flows from the preceding section where it appears in 9:3. This is paralleled with the threefold use of מות (death) in 9:4–5, which is similarly paired with חי in 9:3. The topic of death continues into 9:6 where it is the destroyer of all things, good or ill. The use of קנאה (jealousy) here in 9:6 reminds the reader of the problem of oppression discussed in the only other use of קנאה in 4:1–4, with the retrieval here of something good from death: love, hate and jealousy will be no more. Death is a mixed blessing, in that it will bring an end to evils, but the necessary corollary is that it also means an end to enjoyment.

The conclusion then is to enjoy what can be enjoyed in this life, which would otherwise be spent trying to grasp meaning under the sun. Imperatives typify this section: שתח, אכל, לך (9:7), ראה (9:9) and עשה (9:10), as Qohelet implores his readers to enjoy the life God has given them. Again, as we might expect, the context for this enjoyment is ironically all the vain days of one's life all one's vain days, with הבל twice in construct with (חיי) כל ימי (9:9).[36] Perhaps reinvoking the opening A section, מצא makes another appearance in the final A section, for, although finding out God's purposes may not be within the reach of people, finding good to enjoy under the sun at the hand of God is a good thing for people to do, especially before they end up in *Sheol* (שאול, 9:10).

35. Ogden, *Qoheleth*, 147.
36. See also the similar construction at the beginning of this panel (7:15).

SEEING WHAT QOHELET SAW

9:11–13

This final unit acts as a coda to the whole panel, and as such is much more terse than the other four units. Again this is an ABB`A` unit:

A I turned and **looked** (וראה) under the sun (9:11a)
  B Time doesn't work out the way it should (9:11b)
  B` Time usually works out to be cruel (9:12)
A` **I saw** (ראיתי) this was wisdom under the sun (9:13)

With 9:11–13 the panel is concluded. Unfortunately for the non-Hebrew reader, most English versions make an explicit connection between 9:13 and 14, with the sentence running on between them. This rests on the assumption that what Qohelet saw to be wisdom is found in what happens afterward, whereas according to the structure followed in this book, the חכמה (wisdom) seen under the sun is what was described in the three verses bookended by ראה, namely 9:11–13, not to mention the entire panel which precedes it. Even in those translations where 9:13–14 is not a continued sentence, most translations begin a new paragraph at 9:13, severing the connection between 9:11–12 and 9:13.

Following the logic of the thesis advanced in this book, if the wisdom seen in 9:13 is anaphoric, providing the bookend to 9:11, then Qohelet's reasoning is: I saw, under the sun, that whoever you are, time and chance will happen to you (9:11); I saw, under the sun, that this is wisdom, and this was important to me (9:13).

Both A sections have a first-person verb (שבתי/ראיתי), they both contain ראה, and they both describe the expected location for these investigations: תחת־השמש. Both 9:11a and 9:13 are brief, with Qohelet again coupling ראה with שוב (to turn) to begin a unit in 9:11a (as in 4:1 and also 4:7). The גם which begins 9:13 is probably contrastive: "nevertheless" (cf. Isa 66:3–4).[37] That is, despite the vanity of circumstance, great wisdom nevertheless remains. Indeed, it is in seeing that there is wisdom despite these difficulties is wisdom.

---

37. Koehler and Baumgartner, *Hebrew and Aramaic Lexicon*, s.v. "גַּם".

PART 2: THE OBSERVATION PANELS

Both B sections have patterns within them, which is especially recognizable in the first section. In the rest of 9:11 there is a fivefold chain of לא, which is bookended by clauses beginning with כי: כי לא ... ולא ... וגם לא ... וגם לא ... וגם לא ... כי עת ... :כי. The first כי explains the content of Qohelet's observations, namely, the lack of achievement for effort, while the second one gives the reason for this, namely, time and chance (עת ופגע), which happen to all.

The second B section similarly discusses time (עת), as people (אדם) cannot understand the time (8:12a) because they (אדם) are trapped by time (8:12d). In between these two occurrences of עת, the section is held together through the recurrent י-sound, occurring four times before being ending not with the expected בנים but instead the pattern is broken off with בני האדם.

And yet ("nevertheless"), despite this pessimism, Qohelet has grasped that this is great wisdom (וגדולה היא אלי), for if one can live in light of death and the endless frustration which that brings, then one can truly live.

On its own, it seems as if the unit is lacking the other part of Qohelet's concluding thought. That is, on the one hand, people are not masters of circumstance (a lesson taught from the very outset), but what foil is there to this problem? Qohelet leaves it to the reader to fill this in from what he has already observed and discussed from the preceding four units, namely, that seeking out opportunities to enjoy the gifts God has bestowed on the worker is a key element of what it means to live well in God's world, regardless of whether the time is good or evil.

Summary of 7:15—9:13

Beginning with the opening poem (1:3–11), a looming concern of Ecclesiastes is that people understand their finitude. After all, people have no perspective other than from under the sun; only God can see what occurs under the heavens. But even in that human finitude, there are good things which can be known and embraced, which Qohelet encourages his listeners to heed in this panel.

Unit	OBSERVATION PANEL 4 (7:15—9:13)	
	Use of ראה at the beginning of a unit	Use of ראה at the end of a unit
7:15–28a	ראיתי (7:15)	ראה (7:27)
7:28b—8:9	ראה (7:29)	ראיתי (8:9)
8:10–16	ראיתי (8:10)	לראות (8:16)
8:17—9:10	ראיתי (8:17)	ראה (9:9)
9:11–13	ראה (9:11)	ראיתי (9:13)

Conclusion

In Part 2 of this book we have seen how "I saw" has a crucial role in structuring those sections wherein it is found. Of the forty-seven occurrences of the verb ראה, the main uses of them are in the first person with ראיתי (18x) and אראה (3x), alongside seven infinitives and seven imperatives. Of the twenty-one first-person occurrences of the verb ראה, nineteen of them fall within the observation panels, with the remaining two within the observation interlude (10:5–7),[38] which is also the case for eighty of all the eighty-one first-person verbs in the book.[39]

Therefore, the word and theme associated with "seeing" is clearly a key structuring element in Ecclesiastes, as well as important thematically. For someone to hear what Qohelet says, and to appreciate the wisdom which he has collected (to which we shall shortly turn), they must see what Qohelet sees. The repetition of ראה, and especially ראיתי/אראה, drives the reader back again and again to look with Qohelet at the world around them, that they too might see and comprehend how to live well, among and despite the vanity beheld by all the senses, and primarily what they see with their the eyes.

---

38. We will discuss these verses below in Part 3.

39. Thirty-eight of all the forty-seven occurrences of ראה also fall within the observation panels. Those nine which do not consist of three participles, three imperatives, two infinitives and one 2ms *yiqtol*. The solitary first-person verb which falls outside of the observation panels and interlude is found in 9:16.

PART 3: The Wisdom Collections

The View of the Epilogue Regarding the Rest of the Book

The argument of this book so far has been that half of the body of Ecclesiastes is made up of panels of observation, which in turn can be divided up into units around the verb ראה. The argument pursued in this next part is that those observation panels alternate with wisdom panels, and, taking our cue from the book's epilogue, that these panels are best described as "wisdom collections."

Once the observation panels (as detailed in the previous part) have been bracketed out, what remains are panels which are sapiential in character; indeed, the frame narrator would be surprised were his readers unable to identify any wisdom sayings in all that precedes his conclusion:

> Besides Qohelet being wise, he also taught the people knowledge;
> he weighed and recorded and arranged many proverbs.
> Qohelet sought out delightful words. (12:9–10a)

Rather than a throwaway thought, these verses in the epilogue provide a summary of what the reader should expect to find in the book—not just Qohelet's teaching, but the wisdom he has collected. It is for this reason that the alternating panels are best described as wisdom collections, even though the exact nature of what it means for them to have been "collected" is unclear. They consist of different lengths and forms, but can all in some ways be understood as "wisdom."

Ogden and Zogbo emphasize the breadth of possibilities for understanding the proverbs contained within the book as they (in their handbook for translators) emphasize the importance of retaining the three verbs in the second half of 12:9 (תקן, חקר, אזן) to describe the various activities of finding, selecting, writing, researching, and arranging proverbs.[1] Similarly, Krüger suggests that some sections are "collages" of "contemporary ethical maxims," but admits it is hard to describe the extent to which they are cited word for word and commented upon.[2]

As discussed earlier, Zimmerli has demonstrated that there are parts of Ecclesiastes which correspond to the story form found in Proverbs rather than the short aphorisms alone, which makes identifying the wisdom collections as collected aphorisms problematic. Perhaps it is hard to come much closer than de Jong's "intuitions."[3] As a whole, however, from what has been demonstrated above, a general rule is that the collected wisdom does *not* come in the form of first-person observations, but *does* contain *instruction* (de Jong), *ethics* (Seow) and *aphorisms* (Zimmerli).[4]

In the absence of a more precise description, the overall coherence of the wisdom collections is borne out by the conceptual similarities noted above between the approach taken in this book and the similarities in the description of de Jong, Seow and Zimmerli. In calling the second set of panels wisdom collections, this description is taken from the book itself (12:9–10a). As mentioned above, the terms chosen by others to describe these parts of the book (instruction, ethics and collected sentences) could be more accurately said to describe the content and (part of) the form,

---

1. Ogden and Zogbo, *Handbook on Ecclesiastes*, 435–36.
2. Krüger, *Kohelet (Prediger)*, 250, commenting on 7:1–14.
3. See Part 1 above.
4. See Part 1 above.

PART 3: THE WISDOM COLLECTIONS

while "wisdom" provides the overarching category which is able to encompass all of the material in our wisdom panels. Discussing one section of the wisdom collections (4:17—5:6), Krüger notes that the reader is at this point directly addressed. That is, rather than the first-person narrative, from 4:17 the tone shifts through the use of imperatives, jussives and terse statements, as well as sections that last one to two verses only, such that "die Leser [wird] direkt angesprochen."[5] The discussion in these places is no longer a less personal narrative of Qohelet's undertakings but his exhortations of how to live in light of them. In trying to understand the provenance of these sayings, Krüger explains their presentation (although this time on 7:1–14), writing that "[w]hether present texts or proverbs are literally 'quoted' and 'commented on' can hardly be decided, especially since we must take into account that the text offers its readers pointed caricatures of known positions."[6] But that there are quotes either present *in* the text or at the very minimum *behind* the text is not in question.

Qohelet Among the Sages

There have been three main foci in understanding the sources behind Qohelet's collected wisdom. The first is the rest of the Old Testament, with focus for instance on understanding the sources of Qohelet's creation theology, but especially the other wisdom books of Proverbs and Job. The second has historically been the Greek world, although this has not proven as productive an area of searching.[7] In practice this means that the idea of Greek sources has dropped off the radar in more recent times from a diachronic

---

5. Krüger, *Kohelet*, 206.
6. Krüger and Dean, *Qoheleth*, 135.
7. Although, see Braun, *Kohelet und die Frühhellenistische Popularphilosophie*, 137, where he suggests, "Selbst wenn Kohelet tatsächlich gilgamesch und andere zu seiner Zeit schon sehr alte Literatur gekannt hat, ist damit noch nicht gesagt, daß diese Stoffe ihm nicht durch die hellenistische Bildung vorgelegt wurden." (In other words, just because Qohelet's sources are primarily ancient Near Eastern, this doesn't mean to say that he didn't learn them through a Greek education, with all the influences that implies.)

perspective, being seen to have relevance only from a synchronic perspective.[8] The third source of interest is the literature of the ancient Near East, where some interesting parallels have been unearthed.

In his search for Qohelet's sources in the book of Proverbs, Whybray has suggested four categories of sayings in Ecclesiastes, seeking to cover the breadth of the way in which sayings from earlier traditional wisdom might be used as collections. They are:

1. Sayings which are self-contained: that is, which when considered independently of their contexts express complete thoughts;

2. Sayings which in *form* correspond closely to sayings in Proverbs;

3. Sayings whose *themes* are characteristic of Proverbs, and at the same time in partial or total disagreement or tension either with their immediate contexts or with Qoheleth's characteristic ideas expressed elsewhere in the book;

4. Sayings whose *language* is free from late features such as those of the language of Qoheleth, and is either that of classical Hebrew or more particularly of early wisdom literature.[9]

Whybray goes on to demonstrate that one may make an educated guess at which verses of Ecclesiastes contain a collected wisdom saying rather than a newly invented saying, but certainty would seem to be essentially impossible. After comparing several sayings in Ecclesiastes with the book of Proverbs, he is able to conclude that there are older sayings "which Qohelet incorporated into his book as quotations."[10] Furthermore he is able to demonstrate that "[s]ome of them he quoted with full approval, either making no

---

8. Anderson, "Intertextual Matrix," 157 n. 1; and in a fuller fashion, Jarick, "Ecclesiastes Among the Comedians," 177, who brings Greek comedic texts and Ecclesiastes into an interesting but wholly artificial conversation.

9. Whybray, "Quotations in Ecclesiastes," 437, emphasis original.

10. Whybray, "Quotations," 445.

PART 3: THE WISDOM COLLECTIONS

comment of his own or confirming and elaborating the statements which they make."[11]

An interesting thought experiment (which may become more, should a suitably well-stocked and preserved ancient library of a scribal school be unearthed) is to consider those texts which might conceivably be seen as part of a corpus "collected" by Qohelet into the wisdom panels of Ecclesiastes. Although this is not the focus of this book, and a lot of the work in this area relies on the little that is extant, the possible ways Qohelet may have incorporated his collected wisdom for the wisdom panels includes but is not limited to the following:[12]

1. Quotations (e.g., 4:12, a cord of three is not quickly torn; cf. Epic of Gilgamesh)

2. Paraphrases (e.g., 2:4–9, Qohelet's building accomplishments; cf. Instruction of Amenemhet)

3. Themes (e.g., 2:16, the inevitability of death; cf. Song of Intef)

4. Setting (e.g., 10:16, the importance of the king; cf. Instruction of Amenemhet)

5. Style (e.g., 1:12, 16, 2:1, 15; 3:17, 18: I said to my heart; cf. A man and his *ba'*)

The potential breadth of influence is summed up well by Anderson:

> It seems clear that Ecclesiastes was influenced by the literature of the ancient Near East and on occasion appears to allude to some of it. At other times Ecclesiastes seems to trope it pessimistically. At the very least there are echoes of ancient Near Eastern literature in Ecclesiastes which are consistent with Barton's idea that earlier texts may be simply "in the air."[13]

---

11. Whybray, "Quotations," 445.

12. For references to these and a fuller discussion, see especially Anderson, "Intertextual Matrix."

13. Anderson, "Intertextual Matrix," 175. See his chapter for the details of these ancient Near Eastern texts mentioned above.

Symptomatic of Qohelet's use of these ancient Near East texts (Anderson deals with five in particular) are statements such as, "These clear conceptual and thematic parallels between *Dispute* [*between a man and his* ba'] and Ecclesiastes seem far too close to be coincidences or the general concerns of humanity. It seems that Ecclesiastes was familiar with *Dispute* . . ."[14]

A final inescapable reality is that there is "collected" wisdom, which has not been collected so much as created. Perhaps we could say that the author created it in order to have his muse, Qohelet, collect it. For instance, despite finding parallels with Proverbs and indications of the usage of earlier Israelite wisdom saying, Whybray decides that "[f]or the most part Qoheleth seems to have been unable to find sayings which he could use to express or support his radical teaching, and so he mainly went his own way, guided simply by his personal observation of the world."[15] This seems to go further than the evidence could ever suggest (especially considering the maxim that the absence of evidence does not imply an evidence of absence), and perhaps, had he been able to consider the structure put forward in this book (he lived 1923–1997), might have acknowledged what is primarily original creation in form, in the observation panels, but also what is primarily collected wisdom in form, in the alternate panels.

All this being said, the focus of this book is not on the sources of the wisdom collections, but in how the wisdom collections work as panels, and how they work in conversation with the observation panels. In what follows I will examine the wisdom collections in some detail, before discussing the relationship between the corresponding observation and wisdom panels.

The Four Wisdom Panels in Detail

According to the structure presented in this book, there are four wisdom collections in the book, each of which follow an

---

14. Anderson, "Intertextual Matrix," 163.
15. Whybray, "Quotations," 450.

PART 3: THE WISDOM COLLECTIONS

observation section. Furthermore, a three-part proverb is inserted into the second observation section at 4:5–6 as a wisdom interlude, which nicely reciprocates the observation interlude inserted into the fourth wisdom collection at 10:5–7.[16]

Four wisdom collection panels are thus revealed:

1. Panel 1: 3:1–9
2. Panel 2: 4:17—5:11 [5:1–12]
3. Panel 3: 7:1–14
4. Panel 4: 9:14—11:6

In terms of length, when compared with their corresponding observation panels, they are generally much shorter, with the observation panels ranging from one and a half to three and a half times larger than their corresponding wisdom panel.[17]

Within the four wisdom panels, there are those texts which are more poem-like (e.g., 3:1–9), imperatives to think and act wisely (e.g., 7:13–14), moral stories (e.g., 9:14ff.) and truisms (e.g., 10:8–11). The breadth allows for all the possibilities mentioned above for the origin of the wisdom found in these panels: copied, appropriated, edited and created.

Wisdom Collection 1 (3:1–9)

The first and second observation panels are separated by this brief "Zwischenspiel," dividing the reflections, respectively, of the royal and the wise Qohelet.[18] Structurally, this first wisdom panel can be divided into an introduction and concluding question, which frame a central block of alternatives for which a season will come:

---

16. Both of these interludes will be discussed in detail at the end of this part of the book.

17. Measuring by verses per panel, there are, comparatively and respectively, 33/9, 29/13, 20/14 and 45/31 verses in the observation and wisdom panels.

18. Using the language of Krüger, *Kohelet*, 155.

3:1 Statement: For everything a season
3:2-8 "Sonnet" on time[19]
3:9 Question: Is there any gain?[20]

While this, along with 1:3-11 and 12:1-7, is also self-evidently a poem of sorts,[21] this poem discusses wisdom principles in ways not dissimilar to the other wisdom collections which follow later. In fourteen couplets the reader is presented with contrasting possibilities for action depending on the season, such that none of these options may be described as objectively and always evil, or objectively and always good. Wisdom is, however, about living appropriately according to the situation. This is exemplified in the otherwise contradictory consecutive sayings in Proverbs 26:4-5 (to answer or not to answer a fool?); so too here in 3:2-8 Qohelet presents many more examples of things which, although divisible into desirable and undesirable, each have their time and place under heaven. The reader who would be wise must learn which of these alternatives to choose and when.

In the reality under the sun this will not be easy to determine, because gain is not always evident. As stated prior to this unit, it is not clear what gain there will be for those laboring under the sun (2:22). Qohelet resumes this line of questioning at 3:9, because even if the wise and time-appropriate decision from the alternatives in 3:2-8 is chosen, the reward linked to this wisdom will not necessarily be evident. The question is, is there any gain for the worker in their labor (3:9)? This question remains unanswered, because even when a positive option of those listed in 3:2-8 is the right choice at the right time, the worker knows that a time will surely come when that act must be undone. The doing and inevitable undoing of all things continues to build the feeling of vanity under the sun. That being said, there can be some comfort, as

---

19. This description from Loader, "Qohelet 3:2-8," 240-42.

20. Note also the widely observed inverse correspondence with the opening poem, which opens with a question followed by multiple examples, and concludes with a statement. See for example the table in Krüger, *Kohelet*, 154.

21. Loader, *Polar Structures*, 240-42.

pre-empted in 3:1, knowing this is under God's will. Knowing that there is a time for all things (3:1) provides the assurance that God's heavenly perspective guarantees a fittingness to activities in their time, despite whatever frustrations this causes the people under the heavens. The following observation panel also uses this wisdom panel as a launching-off point, reinforcing the larger perspective which ensures the goodness of these activities even though it may be hard to imagine a time when there will be a right use of the undesirable activities suggested.

Despite the bridge provided by the discussion on time to the observation section which follows in 3:10–15, the point at which our structure would suggest the break is given by the asyndeton ראיתי (3:10).

Relationship between Observation Panel 1 (1:12—2:26) and Wisdom Collection 1 (3:1-9)

As such, the first wisdom collection supports and makes clear the fruitlessness of seeking meaning in worldly achievements—collecting, building, owning. The explanation present in the first wisdom panel is to show that for every desirable outcome, a corresponding undesirable outcome follows and/or will at some stage also have an appropriateness. Just as there might be a time when it is desirable and wise to build, there will be a time when it will be desirable to tear down, even though this is generally seen to be undesirable. Qohelet thus demonstrates that the meaning sought in his building exploits was indeed not going to be found there. If, for everything that might be built, a time will come where it will be just as good to knock it down, then the inability to find meaning in the initial building is frustrated even further through the knowledge that there will come a time for their destruction. The same goes for the vineyards planted as a testimony to Qohelet's greatness—these too will be uprooted, rendering the search for meaning in these exploits all the more futile.

Thus, while there are not perfect analogues in the wisdom panel to all that precedes in the observation panel, the point is well made. The strivings of an individual to pursue meaning on their own will always be shown up in light of God's arbitration over the fittingness and the season.

Wisdom Collection 2 (4:17—5:11 [5:1–12])

This second wisdom panel divides into three paragraphs, each dealing with issues raised in the preceding observation panel. The style of this panel makes it stand out from what precedes it, as Qohelet's first-person observations give way to Qohelet addressing his readers directly.[22] Furthermore, although we have grouped the material here into three, this panel could easily be subdivided into multiple, brief units, which is akin to much of the wisdom found elsewhere, such as in the majority of the book of Proverbs.[23]

> 4:17–5:6 Honor God with your words and deeds
>
> 5:7–8 Oppression is counter to natural (and God's) justice
>
> 5:9–11 If you see oppression, be assured that you can still sleep well

4:17—5:6

The observation panel immediately preceding this (3:10—4:16) discussed both endemic vanity as well as vanity brought on by one's own foolish decisions. This wisdom collection also deals with those concepts, beginning in this unit with self-inflicted vanity. The unit is signaled both by change in tone,[24] but also because it begins and ends with volitives: "guard" (4:17) and "fear" (5:6). The discussion in between them is about both individual decisions as well as a lifestyle which is especially prone to vanity. This has much

---

22. Krüger, *Kohelet*, 206.

23. Krüger, for instance, divides the first nine verses into six separate units of no more than two verses. *Kohelet*, 206.

24. "A new literary unit is signalled by the change in tone. The language of reflection in 4:1–16 gives way to the language of instruction in 5:1–7 (Heb 4:17–5:6)." Seow, *Ecclesiastes*, 197.

more consistency with other parts of the biblical wisdom corpus, with the advice to fear God and to not make vows without thinking or without honoring them. God is not to blame for the vanity experienced through unwise decision-making, as this is wholly the fault of the fool.

A unique contribution here is the idea of dreaming. The content of these dreams is, however, not explained. They are said to come from much work (5:2) and to bring about vanity (5:6), and are set in parallel with the babbling of the fool (5:2). Seow suggests that "dreams" are not necessarily dreams *per se*, but are to be read as synonymous with הבלים (vanities), such that 5:6a is to be read as a hendiadys.[25] 5:2, "For dreams come from much work," could then be the idea that overwork gives rise to vanity, as mentioned in the preceding paragraphs (esp. 4:8).

This first wisdom unit is Qohelet's collected wisdom to warn people away the path of self-imposed vanity. A life which does not revolve around fear of God (5:6c) but is characterized by vain vows, foolish babbling and overwork will meet with God's displeasure (5:5). These sayings are collected by Qohelet to support what he also knows through experience, as he described in the preceding observation panel.

5:7–8

The wisdom panel moves on to discuss endemic structural oppression. As Bartholomew points out,[26] this picks up on themes discussed in the corresponding position in the previous observation panel (4:1–4). The same issue of oppression is picked up on, although (following Bartholomew)[27] 5:7 introduces the saying of 5:8, which shows the unsustainability of such corruption. The king too is dependent on the field, so it can be implied that any power vacuum will affect all who should rightly share in the gain (יתרון)

---

25. Seow, *Ecclesiastes*, 200.
26. Bartholomew, *Ecclesiastes*, 217.
27. Bartholomew, *Ecclesiastes*, 218.

of the field. This works to offset the despair described earlier in 4:1 which could only be loosed in 4:2–3 by death or non-existence. The solution now happened upon is a return to the just rule of God's king to protect the food supply as well as the workers who extract the produce from the land.

Taken together with 4:17—5:6, this unit shows how unwise actions have cumulative negative effects. Not only is God against the fool (5:5–6), but when the fool is in a high position such as that of the king, foolishness works itself out in the form of oppression of the poor and effectively robbery (גזל) of justice and rights, and such injustice affects the whole populace.

5:9–11

Concluding this wisdom collection the theme of foolishness continues with regard to wealth accumulation. This again harks back to 4:7–12, as well as to the preceding wisdom interlude (4:5–6). The question there was whether the single-minded pursuit of wealth was worth it, with the conclusion being that one may have either wealth or friends, but not both. This is reinforced with three sayings on the vanity of wealth accumulation. To paraphrase them:

5:9	Greed seeks to fill a bottomless treasure chest—"this too is vanity"
5:10	The greater the riches, the greater the needs, but the less one can enjoy them[28]
5:11	One can have either wealth or sleep but not both (cf. 4:6)

Important again is the return of the refrain "this too is vanity," which for Qohelet has often described choosing the false or foolish option over a wise option. Pursuing meaning in wealth accumulation is vanity, because they will never be satisfied (5:9), they will not be able to enjoy them (5:10), and they will lose sleep through worry (5:11).

---

28. See Murphy, *Ecclesiastes*, 53.

Qohelet has here skillfully collected and arranged these three proverbs to illustrate what he has observed in the preceding panel: righteous relationship with God and others as a corollary (4:17—5:6), and then wealth as it affects the oppressed (5:7-8) as well as the wealthy (5:9-11).

Relationship between Observation Panel 2 (3:10—4:16) and Wisdom Collection 2 (4:17—5:11)

For the reader who is overwhelmed by the preponderance of evil in the world—which drives enterprise, accompanies the leaders and oppresses the workers—there are some answers found in the observation panel, but also some wise alternatives supplied in the wisdom collection.

There are several hints that the panels are to be read together, for example, the description of the laborer who is able to sleep contrasted with the bottomless pit of greed in 5:10-12 is paralleled in the solution suggested for the friendless workaholic's plight in 4:8-12. So too the wisdom proffered in the face of oppression in 5:8-9 matches the discussion of injustice and oppression in 3:16-22 and 4:1-4.

Both panels recognize injustice; what is described observationally in the second observation panel is matched with corresponding suggestions for wise living in the corresponding wisdom collection.

Wisdom Collection 3 (7:1-14)

This panel follows the third observation panel and is noteworthy for its contrasting character to the observations which precede and follow it. The form of the wisdom found has prompted Krüger to describe this section as something of a "collage" which "deals with contemporary ethical maxims," although what change it may have had from its original form to its being quoted by Qohelet is hard to say ("ist kaum zu entscheiden").²⁹ In terms of its structure, this wisdom panel is again in three parts as follows:

> 7:1–6 What is better in the midst of death
> 7:7–12 What is better than the way of fools
> 7:13–14 Considering what God has made will teach us to live wisely

7:1–6

This first group of sayings has three "better than" (מן ... טוב) expressions and concludes with Qohelet's theme sentence: this too is vanity. The thematic grouping can be illustrated with words about death and life: death, birth (7:1), mourning, living (7:2), grief (7:3) and mourning again (7:4). The final two verses are an expansion of the conclusion to 7:4; appropriate behavior in the house of mourning is here substituted by the song and laughter of fools.

7:7–12

The second group continues the contrast between wisdom and folly with the route from wisdom to foolishness. Extortion, bribery (7:7), pride (7:8), anger (7:9) and living in the past (7:10) are all ways to turn a wise person into a fool. Wisdom is as good as, if not better than, an inheritance and money (7:11–12).

7:13–14

These two verses conclude this wisdom collection and transition to the following observation panel. There are three imperatives, two of which implore the reader with ראה to "see" (or consider) what God has done. The reader is implored to gain a proper perspective by looking at God and his works. These act as a coda to the preceding paragraphs, to reinforce the message that there is a

---

29. Krüger, *Kohelet*, 250.

greater reality than death and omnipresent fools, in the inscrutable and everlasting God. Wisdom will not enable people to fix all that is broken in the world or correct every fool. But it will enable them to live appropriately for the times God has placed them in, mourning when things are not going well, but also being able to rejoice in those times of good bestowed by the creator on his creatures.

Relationship between Observation Panel 3 (5:12—6:12) and Wisdom Collection 3 (7:1–14)

Rather than the depressing acknowledgement in the first wisdom collection that both desirable and undesirable alternatives will at some time be the wise choice whatever we pursue, the third panels discuss what is good and evil. The third observation panel says that much evil has been seen: 5:12, 13, 15; 6:1, 2. In the middle unit, however (5:17–19), there is a description of the good things Qohelet has seen: הנה אשר־ראיתי אני טוב. Qohelet has indeed seen good things, and in wisdom collection 3, which follows, those good or better things are discussed (7:1, 2, 3, 5, 8, 10, 11). This continues throughout wisdom collection 3 until 7:14, when the conclusion is made that there are good days and evil days, and God has made both of them. Qohelet's wisdom concludes that a good day should be enjoyed, while on a bad day all that can be offered is to remember that God is God.

Between observation panel 3 and wisdom collection 3 there is a linguistic link, with the words "good" and "evil" dominating both panels. Yes, there is much evil, but God still gives humanity good, and gives them better alternatives to embrace and enjoy on those good days that are granted to them.

Wisdom Collection 4 (9:14—11:6)

As discussed above, this panel could properly continue until 11:10, although 11:7–10 is best understood as a wisdom introduction to 12:1–7, as discussed below. This panel is easily the longest wisdom collection of the book, and contains within it the observation interlude at 10:5–7 and leads into the wisdom introduction to the final poem. It divides into three units as follows:

9:14–10:4	Might does not mean right
10:5–7	Observation interlude[30]
10:8–20	Negative examples of act-consequence
11:1–6	Limitations of human knowledge

9:14—10:4

Between the observation panel concluding at 9:13 and the observation interlude (10:5–7), Qohelet has collected a series of proverbs which illustrate how something small can make a difference against something much larger. He relates the story of a small city with few men and only one poor but wise man; through him they triumphed against a great king with his great siegeworks (9:14–15). Perhaps predictably, his name was forgotten (9:15), and, as Qohelet interjects, more often than not such people wouldn't even gain a hearing (9:16). Despite Qohelet's experience and even against the lack of recognition given the wise man in the parable, he still compiles further examples to prove the goodness of the small and the wise. Sometimes this is a positive example (9:17, 18a; 10:4), but sometimes negative (9:18b; 10:1). The folly of the mighty also provides the occasion for the observation interlude as the poor choices of the king leave the kingdom in disarray (10:5–7).

10:5–7

Within this final wisdom panel, the aphoristic character is broken with the first and second (and also final) appearance of ראיתי/ אראה since the preceding observation panel.[31] As with many other

---

30. Also observed by Bartholomew, *Ecclesiastes*, 323.
31. The three remaining occurrences of ראה in the book are as a participle

units found within observation panels, this interlude begins and ends with ראיתי, giving an ABA` structure.

> A **I saw** (ראיתי) an evil under the sun resulting from foolish rulers (10:5)
> B Fools are elevated while the rich are demoted (10:6)
> A` **I saw** (ראיתי) that the places of slaves and princes have been confused (10:7)

As we have been trained to expect by this point in Ecclesiastes, the presence of ראיתי indicates the observations of Qohelet, which in this case are the results, under the sun, of the errors of foolish rulers. 10:5 lists this as the cause, and describes this as a great evil (cf. 5:12; 6:1). The evidence of this is again what he has seen (10:7), where the rightful places of slaves and masters have been switched, with slaves on horseback (עבדים על־סוסים) while their rulers go about, as should their servants, on the ground (ושרים הלכים כעבדים על־הארץ). There are some similarities here to the description of those following the ruler in 4:13–16, in particular the context of the foolish ruler and the manner of those walking about. In 10:7 they walk upon the earth (הלכים ... על־הארץ), but in 4:15 they walk under the sun (המהלכים תחת השמש). In both circumstances the presence of the ruler is depicted negatively.

The center of the unit (10:6) explains the evil (10:5) which led to this situation (10:7), namely, fools are given high positions, while the "rich" (עשירים) are given lowly positions. The wealthy receive a repeated focus in Ecclesiastes. Later in the same chapter the parallelism implies they are to be understood as one and the same as the king (10:20). And yet, because wealth is a gift of God (5:18; 6:2), the misuse of this wealth, especially by the rulers, is especially galling and incomprehensible to Qohelet. This contrasts with the presentation elsewhere of the wealthy with those who have wisdom and prudence (cf. Ps 112:3; Prov 14:24).

The problem observed by Qohelet is that the ones who have the wisdom, experience and knowledge of good management and

---

in 11:4, an infinitive in 11:7 and another participle in 12:3.

public service are given neither respect (10:7) nor authority to govern (10:6). This is an evil under the sun which stems from the mismanagement of the ruler. Qohelet is not here (necessarily) advocating an end to the concept of monarchy, but longs for a return to the just and wise rule of kings.

10:8–20

The second group of proverbs in this section provides by far the most random collection of the book, yet at the same time the most orthodox. Several may be grouped together: 10:8–10 speaks of cause and effect; 10:11–14 is concerned with thinking before speaking; 10:15 stands on its own; and 10:16–20 seems related to royal leadership. What perhaps unites them is they each provide examples of where things could or will go wrong (although note that the CSB translates them modally, and the ESV as likely probabilities). They could each be reworked as helpful warnings (don't dig a pit; don't use blunt iron; only perform with a charmed snake?!), but more likely, considering the tone of the book as a whole, are larger scale examples of vanity, stitched into creation.[32]

There is a tension created here by the elevation of the mighty over the fool, while Qohelet has previously demonstrated the folly of trusting in rulers over the poor yet wise. The answer lies somewhere in between, as new royals may be foolish and it would be foolish to put one's trust in such a ruler, while the king mentioned here as worthy of praise knows how to run a kingdom and those under him (10:16–17).

A further point of tension is raised in 10:19, where for the first time a *carpe diem* statement is completed with money being praised.

---

32. These examples perhaps most closely describe the doctrine of a fallen creation as expressed in Romans 8:20, where the Greek ματαιότης represents the Hebrew הבל.

לשׂחוק עשׂים לחם	Food makes for laughter,
ויין ישׂמח חיים	wine gladdens life,
והכסף יענה את־הכל:	and money answers everything.

There are, however, differences between this and the other *carpe diem* statements, as well as difficulties with the verse itself. The other statements are found in observation panels rather than wisdom collections, which may partly explain why they are different to 10:19. However, there is also a difference in vocabulary and syntax. Elsewhere there is an instruction ("there is nothing better than...," "go ahead and...") and the verbs eat and drink, whereas the verbs here describe the result of bread and wine. Perhaps there is some merit to Seow's suggestion that ענה is to be translated here following the Syriac as a *hiphil* ("preoccupied") rather than a *qal* ("answers"),[33] ostensibly with a disjunctive *waw* as well, which would lead to the sense of "food and wine bring joy, but money preoccupies everything." This would then be contrasting the goodness of enjoying food and wine with the dangers of greed (cf. 4:8). The alternative, however, is not to read this as a *carpe diem* statement at all, due to the difference in syntax and vocabulary as mentioned above, but as a proverb collected by Qohelet which actually does praise the positive uses of money.

Ultimately, one can either follow Bartholomew, who reads this as a commendation of the goodness of wise kings, with money enabling them to govern, to gain strength through timely and moderate eating and drinking[34]; or one can take Seow's view, reading the final clause as a contrast. Although the contrast fits with much of what Qohelet has said, Bartholomew's "[ironic] twist" is appealing.[35] The contrast is then not an absolute between poverty and riches, where poverty is linked with wisdom and riches with

---

33. Seow, *Ecclesiastes*, 332.
34. Bartholomew, *Ecclesiastes*, 326.
35. Bartholomew, *Ecclesiastes*, 326.

folly, but riches under the control of the wise is the only appropriate place for them.

In this unit Qohelet both uses and subverts traditional wisdom by mixing the traditional categories. This is reminiscent of the first wisdom collection in chapter 3, where both desirable and undesirable actions had their good place—frustrating as that is to people—in God's timing.

11:1-6

The final unit collects proverbs which link the idea that human knowledge is limited. Among these are those with the "x, x+1" formula in 11:2 (cf., e.g., Job 5:19; Prov 6:16). In verses 1-2 and 5-6 Qohelet uses the second-person masculine address, perhaps for emphasis,[36] although it may more likely be an unremarkable poetic device. Whatever the case, the point is this: because people are limited by mortal ignorance, there is a way to live that responds to what Qohelet has taught throughout the book. Interesting here is the possible idea of a life—yes, a life lived in ignorance, but nonetheless a life well lived—that not only receives as gift but also lives graciously in return. As they have freely received, so they can freely sow their seed, they can work at their labor (11:6), even though "you don't know the work of God who makes everything" (11:5c).

Relationship between Observation Panel 4 (7:15—9:13) and Wisdom Collection 4 (9:14—11:6)

The final two panels both describe God as maker. In observation panel 4, Qohelet has seen that God is the one who made (עשׂה) people upright, despite their own decisions to go astray. In wisdom collection 4, God is again the one who made (יעשׂה) all things; he is the only one who has perfect knowledge. And this description

---

36. Bullinger, *Figures of Speech*, 524.

of God is the overarching reality which relativizes the many issues which plague these final panels of the book.

The problem of ignorance is present throughout both of these panels. Qohelet saw that the rewards appropriate for the righteous and wicked are often confused. The collected wisdom similarly presents a confused world. The question which hovers over these panels is whether it is right to pursue wisdom. In the observation panels, Qohelet admits that no amount of wisdom will ever allow people to fully comprehend God's ways. In the wisdom collections, there are exhortations towards wisdom, but equally there are counterexamples described: anti-wisdom.

However, Qohelet never loses sight of the bigger picture, that God is God, which for him means that even finite humans are allowed to enjoy God's good gifts and to embrace the life they've been given. And so, despite the confusion which is rife, there is still a place for wisdom, for choosing a wise path, even when the hoped-for results of wise choices are not assured.

Summary of the Relationship between Observation and Wisdom Panels

It would be untrue and indefensible to claim that the panels are perfect analogues of each other, or that for each observation one can find a matching aphorism. However, by following the structure I have described, the appropriateness of juxtaposing the observation panels and the wisdom collections can be seen.

The first pair demonstrate the vanity in seeking meaning through achievement. The second pair focus on injustice, both observed and through wisdom sayings. The third pair look at the reality of an evil world, and in that context see where good can be found. The final pair speak a word reminiscent of the conclusion, of fearing God and enjoying his gifts, despite the ignorance plaguing humankind.

The panels have been carefully arranged and the wisdom thoughtfully curated in order to complement Qohelet's observations. Rather than a book with no order, Ecclesiastes is ordered with its panels in order to "guide readers in recognizing and remembering the author's train of thought[.]"[37]

The Two Interludes

Despite the order observed and described by the two sets of alternating panels, there are two exceptions which stand out as breaking the pattern, namely:

- The wisdom interlude (4:5-6) within the second observation panel (3:10-4:16);
- The observation interlude (10:5-7) within the fourth wisdom panel (9:14-11:6).

The question to be examined in this final section of this third part of this book is what these five verses are doing and what can explain their placement outside their panels.

4:5-6

Ecclesiastes 4:5-6 presents a classic example of a *via media*, with the two extremes framing the desirable third way:[38]

הכסיל חבק את־ידיו ואכל את־בשרו:
טוב מלא כף נחת
ממלא חפנים עמל ורעות רוח:

"The fool folds their hands and eats their flesh (4:5), [but] it is better [to have] a full hand [with] rest (4:6a) than full handfuls [from] toil but striving after wind (4:6b)." The one extreme is sloth, leaving the only source of food being their own body (cf. Prov 21:25). The converse extreme is to have much to eat resulting from much

---

37. Fox, *Time to Tear Down*, 149.

38. As discussed above, I see these two verses as describing two extremes and a *via media*, although it could be argued that 4:5 presents one situation, while 4:6 describes a mutually informing, yet distinct, situation with a טוב . . . מן construction (cf. for instance Athas, *Ecclesiastes, Song of Songs*).

PART 3: THE WISDOM COLLECTIONS

toil, but this is seen to be vain, equivalent to chasing the wind. This *via media* takes the best from both alternatives, namely, enough work to have enough food, but not so much work that there is no rest available.

These two verses with their two extremes and one mediating path are expressed with appropriate terseness, with the extremes having five words, while the third way is expressed with only four words. There are no active verbs either; the only verbal forms are the two participles in 4:5 (חבק and אכל), which is another common aphoristic attribute. These verses are closely intertwined, each assuming the existence of the other. The first introduces the idea of extreme rest, folding one's hands and doing nothing. This idea of rest is developed with one of those hands not being folded but working to be full. In turn this fullness is taken further, with the development from both folded, to one resting and one working, to finally both being full from toil, but no mention of rest.

What can be seen then is that this triplet is clearly aphoristic in form, but also that it contrasts with the first-person narrative surrounding it. Immediately before and following 4:5–6 are two blocks of observation and conclusion framed as the observations of Qohelet. There is a completeness in what is said there, as has been discussed above in the section on the observation panels. The question is, then, why has this wisdom interlude been included here rather than with the wisdom panel which follows, in 4:17—5:11? One answer could be that it should be, and that we should relocate the passage, perhaps after 5:8, which would fit the new context well. But working with the principle of understanding the text as received, the answer instead is to understand why it is where it is.

There are three main reasons why 4:5–6 is best understood as a wisdom interlude that has deliberately been placed in its current location within an observation panel. The first is for emphasis: it stands out. In the midst of units beginning and ending with "I saw," this short aphorism draws attention to itself because of its apparent dislocation. As the reader stops to consider whether it properly belongs with the preceding or following unit, they have read the aphorism many times over, and have therefore begun the process of reflecting in light of the interlude, which is indeed the purpose of wisdom literature.

The second reason relates to the linguistic link to the preceding verse, 4:4, which also finishes with רעות רוח (striving after wind, 4:6), such that the reader is immediately introduced to a further evidence(s) of vanity under the sun.[39] It is, however, a different instance of vanity, but it is the same as the following half-unit, namely, 4:7–12.

This leads to the third reason, that the wisdom interlude is inserted at this point to introduce the observation of workaholism of the next unit. This adds to the impact of the unit, by essentially teaching the same truth in two different ways, first as a wisdom saying, and secondly as an observation with its conclusion: it is better to have a friend with whom one may share their wealth than to endlessly toil in solitude.

10:5–7

Mirroring the placement of a wisdom interlude in an observation panel (4:5–6), there is similarly an observation interlude in a wisdom collection (10:5–7):

יש רעה ראיתי תחת השמש כשגגה שיצא מלפני השליט:
נתן הסכל במרומים רבים ועשירים בשפל ישבו:
ראיתי עבדים על־סוסים ושרים הלכים כעבדים על־הארץ:

As with the second and fourth observation units in the book, this interlude is framed with language of observation: "I saw." This would otherwise be the shortest observation panel in the book, hence the title "interlude." Qohelet gives a description of an evil that he has seen under the sun.[40] The first verse gives the context: this is an evil that has been observed by Qohelet, and it relates to

---

39. All the instances of this phrase in the book (and indeed in the whole Bible) are found in the observation panels (1:14; 2:11, 17, 26; 4:4, 6; 6:9).

40. See also the similar constructions in 5:12; 6:1.

PART 3: THE WISDOM COLLECTIONS

his observation of a situation in which "'inadvertently' (perhaps Qohelet is deliberately ironic) a ruler allows the world to be turned upside down."[41] The wider context dictates that this should be discussing how to live wisely under a monarchy, with the opening illustration about rulers versus the poor (9:14–18), fools and rulers (10:3–4), noble-born and lower-caste kings (10:16–17) and perhaps even rulers (10:20).[42]

What is observed and described in 10:6–7 is a topsy-turvy kingdom, where every day is "opposites day."[43] Qohelet has seen the positions of fools and slaves interchanged, respectively, with the rich and princes. For Qohelet this is symptomatic of an absence of wise leadership, and he does not like what he has seen.

As with the wisdom interlude discussed above, this observation interlude similarly serves its immediate context by introducing an anecdote from Qohelet's experience. What he has observed with his eyes corresponds with the wisdom he has assembled regarding life in a monarchy (as the king, so are the subjects). By this point in the book the reader is well accustomed to noting the change from wisdom to observation and back again, so this interlude will stand out and cause the attentive reader to pause and consider what they themselves have seen.

These two short sections examined, rather than being the exceptions which prove the rule, demonstrate Qohelet's commitment to his structure of alternating observation and wisdom panels, by using these two interludes to reinforce the points being made in those places. They both clearly break the structure of the units either side of them, but nonetheless have clear linguistic and thematic links. These two short interludes, 4:5–6 and 10:5–7, stand out in order to highlight the importance of what has been said, in the first place, regarding a right understanding of work, and in the second, regarding orderly rule.

---

41. Bartholomew, *Ecclesiastes*, 322.
42. Bartholomew, *Ecclesiastes*, 320.
43. Or perhaps Qohelet is imagining a tradition similar to that associated with Boxing Day, where the roles of masters and servants are inverted for a day.

Summary

The wisdom collections together demonstrate the prevalence and importance of this second type of discourse: wisdom. While often disparate sayings, some coherence among them can be seen, and moreover a degree of correspondence with the observation panels is also evident. The symbiotic relationship between the two types of discourse—the first-person narrative in the observation panels, and the aphorisms in the wisdom collections—demonstrates that the body of the book has a structure which governs the placement of material. The wisdom collections are to be read in response to what has been described in Qohelet's first-hand experiences, and that context is to govern their reading.

The exceptions of 4:5–6 and 10:5–7 are noteworthy because they stand out, which demonstrates that there is an established norm from which they have deviated. Were there no structure, they would not be remarkable. As it is, they are, reinforcing the conversation between Qohelet's observations and his collected wisdom.

PART 4: The Book's Bookends

As mentioned earlier, Reinert helpfully describes the beginning and end of the book as the "Äusserer" and "Innerer Rahmen,"[1] or the outer and inner borders—the book's bookends. This language is conceptually identical to my own, which is why I mention him at this point. That being said, his contents are narrower than mine, as he excludes the poems from these and separates the "Motto" (1:2; 12:8) away from the verses surrounding them. This leaves him with an outer border of 1:1; 12:9-14 and an inner border of 1:2; 12:8, whereas I have combined these as 1:1-2; 12:8-14, as will be explained below. He calls each poem (along with 3:1-8) a "Maschal" (1:4-11; 11:7—12:7), although this meaning is slightly at odds with the use of משל within Ecclesiastes (12:9) to mean proverb.[2]

I will retain similar language, describing the two poems (1:3-11; 11:7—12:7) as internal bookends and, by grouping the motto (1:2; 12:8) with the verses external to it, describe the introduction and conclusion as the external bookends (1:1-2; 12:8-14). In what follows I will explain why I include the motto with the introduction and conclusion, and what that means for the role it plays there, as well as for the book as a whole. I will also discuss how the internal and external bookends shape the way we read the book as alternating panels of observation and wisdom. For easy reference, the important parts of the structure referred to here are:

1. Reinert, *Salomofiktion*, 37ff.
2. See the clear structure diagram in Reinert, *Salomofiktion*, 169.

1:1–2 Opening external bookend (motto at 1:2)
   1:3–11 Opening internal bookend
      1:12–11:6 Alternating panels of observation and wisdom
   11:7–12:7 Concluding internal bookend
12:8–14 Concluding external bookend (motto at 12:8)

The Internal Bookends

The opening and closing poems each deal with the biggest topics there are: in the first, the place of humanity in a vast and unrelenting universe; in the second, human decay which inevitably leads to death. In what follows I will discuss the structure and meaning of each of these and consider how they set the tone of Qohelet's investigations.

Opening Poem on Life in the Context of the Cosmos (1:3–7)

The opening poem[3] begs a question which will be returned to repeatedly throughout the book: what can anyone ever gain from anything they do? Preceded as it is by the skepticism of the Solomon figure (1:1–2), the book begins with a tone of exasperation. The poem goes through various examples to demonstrate how minute humans are in contrast with the cosmos—the earth is immovable, the sun never stops moving, the wind is untamable, the cycle of precipitation goes on and on—yet people are here one minute and gone the next. There are echoes of Job 28 here and perhaps even a nihilistic retelling of Psalm 8. And yet, there is something about humans. Yes, the human lifespan is pitiable when compared with the vastness of the cosmos, but nevertheless, humans persist. So too human senses—finite they might be, yet paradoxically they cannot be filled. However, rather than giving Qohelet cause for optimism, his conclusion (1:9–11) shows that

---

3. For the reasons this can and should be called a poem, see Bartholomew, *Ecclesiastes*, 111.

trying to find meaning in these things is a vain pursuit. Indeed, rather than being impressed with the ability to receive seemingly endless sensory input, the conclusion is that "all the words are weary" (11:8a). Disappointment, rather than excitement about human abilities, is the conclusion from this comparison.

As a poem which opens the book, it prepares the ground well for what will follow. On the one hand, there are things which are permanent, and then on the other, there are humans and human achievements. Nothing anyone adds will last, and nothing anyone does will be new, and no achievement anyone boasts in will be remembered. The question is, then again, where can meaning be found in this impossible cosmos, with the few years assigned to people under the sun? That question will be at the forefront of Qohelet's discussions throughout the book.

A structure presents itself as follows:

A The question (1:3)

  B The paradox of humans on the earth: in flux yet the earth is firm (1:4)

    C The example of the sun: always moving (1:5)

      D The example of the wind: untamable (1:6)

    C` The example of the water: always moving (1:7)

  B` The paradox of the senses: never satisfied yet weary from sensing (1:8)

A` Statement in response to the question (1:9–11)

Although there is not too much to read into this structure (except perhaps to note the parallels), the persistent question raised is where meaning is to be found in a world where people have so little control over their surrounds.

Concluding Poem of Life in the Context of Death (11:7—12:7)

The connection between 11:7-10 and 12:1-7 is self-evident. 11:7-10 commends the benefits and opportunities of youth, to be enjoyed while the possibilities for youthful enjoyment are still there. The contrast is then set up with what follows from 12:1, as those opportunities of youth will not be there once one has reached their old age. There is some discussion over whether the whole section is to be thought of as a poem, or only 12:1-7. Bartholomew takes this whole section as a poem, although he does begin by describing the beginning as a "proverb"; he and those he references also note the togetherness of 11:7—12:7/8, but also a clear change from 11:7-10 to 12:1-7/8.[4] Considering 11:7-10 in context, an argument could be made to connect it with the wisdom collection which precedes it, although of course that would sever the connection between what follows in 12:1ff. In that light, it seems best to consider the whole of 11:7—12:7 as one section, but within that to read 11:7-10 as a wisdom introduction to the poem "proper" of 12:1-7.[5]

Of the three options described by Fox,[6] I understand the various illustrations of a village in decline as an allegory of what happens to a person as they age, as various functions of the body are increasingly impaired, culminating in 12:7 with death.[7] As with the impassibility of the cosmos in 1:3-11, the steady march of

---

4. Bartholomew, *Ecclesiastes*, 343. It should also be noted that 12:8 appears among commentators variously as the conclusion to the poem, standing alone, or with the epilogue.

5. Parallels could perhaps be made with the observation conclusion in 3:10-15 to what precedes and follows it. In that place I chose for formal structural reasons to include it with the observation panel which followed rather than as an observation conclusion to the preceding wisdom collection which it references. In this case, neither option is wrong, but failing any other arguments I believe the section 11:7—12:7 is the most defensible.

6. Fox, *Ecclesiastes*, 76-77, who adopts a multivalent reading encompassing each of the three readings: allegorical, literal and eschatological.

7. My tentative interpretation understands the following images: 12:2 eyes, 12:3 face (lips, cheeks, teeth, eyes), 12:4 hearing, 12:5 stomach, 12:6 frame (spinal cord, head, torso, legs), 12:7 death.

PART 4: THE BOOK'S BOOKENDS

decline leading to death is inescapable. The advice of 12:1 is therefore all the more pressing: listen and respond to God while you still can, before your ears no longer hear and your eyes no longer see.

The contrast between the two theme words of this section, "rejoice" and "remember,"[8] is apposite for this concluding poem. People are enjoined to rejoice while they can (as in 11:7–10) and are cautioned to remember the decline to come, especially in the context of death (as in 12:1–7). As such, the poem draws out and reinforces two of the key ideas evident in the rest of the book.

The poem itself has the following structure:

A Death will come, so remember your creator (12:1)
  B When the eyes fail (12:2)
    C When the face degrades (12:3)
      D When the hearing stops working (12:4)
    C` When the stomach degrades (12:5)
  B` When the frame fails (12:6)
A` Death will come (12:7)

The key thing for this structure is the frame, as the most important point is filled out: death will come, so the only opportunity to choose well is while you still live. Qohelet has had differing views on death. At times, especially when confronted by injustice, he prefers it to life (4:1–4; 6:3), but at other times life is precious and worth holding onto at any cost (7:17; 9:4–5). At any rate, no decisions can be made after death, only during one's lifetime. Hence, at the center, the description of the loss of hearing, where there is no slamming of doors, no grinding at the mill, and even birdsong grows faint. This may well be compared with the king in 4:13 who longer heeds warning; he is old, foolish, and is either unwilling or unable to hear—or perhaps even both.

The wise decision people should make is to "remember your creator" (12:1); while the experience for Qohelet throughout the book has been that "remembering your creator" may not

---

8. Bartholomew, *Ecclesiastes*, 345.

necessarily lead to advantageous outcomes, it is still best to do so, for gifts only come—if they do indeed come—from the hand of God.

The Complementary Shape of the Internal Bookends

The important structural role these two poems play in the book, giving shape as the internal bookends, similarly give shape to the experience of life observed by Qohelet within the book. As good and as noble as people may be elsewhere in the Scriptures (cf., e.g., Gen 1–2; Ps 8), the realities encountered in Ecclesiastes, and the lack of impact any person is able to exert under the sun, show that people are in matter of fact small, impotent and ineffective. Those things that will be have been before, those things that could be built will be torn down. And all the while people go about under the sun, watching fools gain power only to wield it to the harm of their fellow human.

This beginning perspective matches the corresponding concluding bookend, as it provides a full stop to the book akin to its subject: death. The pursuit of justice is frustrated by death (either the wrongdoer or the one seeking justice); so too all achievements are relativized by death and the lottery of inheritance. The endless coming and going of generations (1:4), punctuated as they are by the regularity of the deaths of everyone under the sun, add to the accumulation of הבל—Qohelet's noted inability to grasp hold of meaning through pursuits under the sun.

It is worth noting the similarities in the style of the poems, especially the tendency to list multiple contributing examples. This is also evident throughout the book, for instance in 2:1–11, in the pairs in 3:1–9, just as here with the multiple illustrations of the same points in 1:3–11 and 12:1–7. Although there may be escalations (esp. in 2:1–11) or a central focus, the purpose is always cumulative. This speaks to the aim of the book being not to present a hopeful journey from ignorance to enlightenment, but to describe and investigate the realities of life under the sun—the

PART 4: THE BOOK'S BOOKENDS

endlessly repeating problems and questions which accost each and every person in each and every generation.

The External Bookends

One thing that is in clear agreement in Qohelet studies is the existence of an external frame, even though its specific boundaries are still being debated. Fox explains that "most commentators regard the epilogue (12:9–14) as an appendix added by a later scribe or 'editor.'"[9] Despite this, it seems best to read the whole book as a unitary work, for reasons briefly outlined in the introduction.[10] This view understands the frame to have been written by the same hand as the rest of the book.[11] Not to minimize the importance of the question of the number of authors for how the book is interpreted, there is agreement that the book presents itself as comprising (at the very least) an introduction, body and conclusion. What is not so clear is where the lines should be drawn between the frame and the body of the book. Further complicating matters is the refrain just inside the frame (1:2; 12:8), which repeats the motto, leading to the question of whether it makes sense for the frame narrator to report this phrase, or does it fit better with the body of the book, as the narrator handing over to and then taking over from Qohelet? As has been briefly discussed above and will be discussed below, it seems best to include the motto with the introduction and conclusion to the words of Qohelet, as part of the external bookends.[12] In this I come to agree with the sentiments expressed by Reinert

---

9. Fox, *Ecclesiastes*, xvii.

10. Fox and Shead are two examples of those who read the whole as authorship rather than editorship. Fox, *Ecclesiastes*, 83; Shead, "Reading Ecclesiastes 'Epilogically.'"

11. For recent authors who see clear contradiction between Qohelet and the frame narrator, see the scathing rebuttal to Shead by Shields, "Ecclesiastes and the End of Wisdom," and the more even-handed opinion of Longman, who sees Qohelet as a real person rather than a literary persona. Longman, *Book of Ecclesiastes*, 9.

12. See also Longman, *Book of Ecclesiastes*, 275, who bases this division on the change from first person (address) to third person (narration).

that if one were to continue the words of the character of Qohelet beyond 4:16 (the point at which, for him, the "Salomofiktion" ends), then 12:7 is the logical point at which his words end and the narrator again takes over the reins.[13]

Introduction to Qohelet's Words (1:1–2)

The opening two verses of the book do two things. They introduce the speaker, Qohelet, who is to be understood as in the line of David, with great power in Jerusalem. This speaker is paired with his message: the words of Qohelet (1:1)—vanity of vanities (1:2). 1:1–2 is then a summary of how to read the book and what to look out for. 1:1–2 introduces Qohelet as one who will speak with the resources and opportunities and wisdom of someone who is at least as great as (if not greater than) Solomon, and vanity will be the focus of his investigations.

As far as an introduction goes, this is a paradox. On the one hand, the observations detailed within the book are to be read as the investigations of a great king, but on the other hand, everything is vanity. The frustration of having on one hand all the resources possible, yet with the other not being able to grasp on to meaning, is the riddle which will be embraced and dissected throughout the book. That "all" (הבל) is vanity does not necessarily pre-empt the outcome of the investigations, but rather indicates that the very searching for meaning will in itself be an act of vanity and, even while trying to find a solution, in some way contribute to the confusion of seeking out meaning in a vain and cruel world.

The opening then presents a pattern of reading, of two alternative positions or perspectives (or, perhaps, following Loader, "poles") on the same reality. As per the thesis of this book, those two perspectives of observation and wisdom are presented throughout Ecclesiastes, and are to be expected, at least in retrospect, from reading the introduction to Qohelet's words in 1:1–2.

---

13. Reinert, *Salomofiktion*, 177.

PART 4: THE BOOK'S BOOKENDS

Conclusion to Qohelet's Words (12:8–14)

The concluding external bookend is much longer and more expansive than the first. The refrain at 12:8 echoes that in 1:2, with minimal differences (it does not repeat הבל הבלים, while קהלת gains a definite article). However, the thought in 12:8 is expanded upon in 12:12b, which provides a description of vanity, albeit without the word הבל. There is also a repeated phrase, "and in addition" (ויתר), beginning both 12:9 and 12:12, while in 12:10 and 12:11 there is a characteristic polar tension, where Qohelet—who is wise (12:9)—sought out good (or delightful) words or sayings, and yet sayings of the wise are goads (12:11; cf. the discussion above around 1:1–2). This points toward the following ABCC`B`A` structure, with a concluding couplet (DD`):

A Everything is vanity (12:8)
  B In addition Qohelet was wise and taught (12:9)
    C Qohelet sought out good sayings (12:10)
    C` Sayings of the wise are goads (12:11)
  B` In addition be warned my son (12:12a)
A` Books and study are vanity (12:12b)
      D All is heard—fear God and obey his commandments (12:13)
      D` God will judge everything (12:14)

The center of the concentric structure of 12:8–12 matches the approach of the whole book: these are good and wise (even delightful) words, but they hurt. They present an uncomfortable reality, but grappling with that reality will ultimately benefit anyone under the sun who will heed the experiences and teaching of Qohelet.

The final two verses (12:13–14) are brief and terse, yet are able to summarize the book as a whole. These verses also provide a counterpoint to the first section of the epilogue; while the first section reflects on Qohelet and what he could discern under the sun, the second reflects on God and what he reveals under the heavens. The concise Hebrew could be represented in English as follows:

סוֹף דָּבָר הַכֹּל נִשְׁמָע	Matter's end, all's heard.
אֶת־הָאֱלֹהִים יְרָא וְאֶת־מִצְוֺתָיו שְׁמוֹר	Fear God, commands keep.
כִּי־זֶה כָּל־הָאָדָם׃	This = man.
כִּי	*for*
אֶת־כָּל־מַעֲשֶׂה הָאֱלֹהִים יָבִא בְמִשְׁפָּט	God judges all works:
עַל כָּל־נֶעְלָם	all secrets,
אִם־טוֹב וְאִם־רָע׃	good & bad.

As such, the כִּי (for) in the center of the two verses provides the hinge, and we know that this is the end of what we will hear from Qohelet. The narrator has not contradicted Qohelet, but has drawn the threads together, concluding that it is right and wise to fear the God who will bring everything into judgment.

Moreover, the two halves of the epilogue provide an important counterpoint to each other. As Andrew Shead explains,

> When we read the observation "All is vanity" together with the imperative "Fear God", we do not end up with orthodox legal piety, but with a radical synthesis of despair and hope.[14]

The book concludes by reminding us again that vanity is omnipresent, and yet there is wisdom to be found and to follow. This wisdom begins, as Proverbs often reminds the reader, with fearing the God who will judge. What matters, then, is not what one has gained or achieved, since there is no true gain under the sun. Rather, it is how one has responded to the goads of wisdom, given to all constrained to live their vain life under the sun, which matters to the God who created both sun and everything under it.

As discussed earlier, and noted by Seow, the appellation "Qohelet," combined with "the words of," at times introduces a prophet.[15] Although Qohelet is more naturally associated with a king (son of David, king over Israel in Jerusalem, 1:1, 12), it is an interesting thought experiment to think of Qohelet in prophetic terms. His words are rarely comforting, but are truly goad-like. He

---

14. Shead, "Reading Ecclesiastes 'Epilogically,'" 90.
15. Seow, *Ecclesiastes*, 98.

has seen firsthand that many are the roads to vanity, and with continued references to death and people's vaporous grip on meaning, he seeks to shock the reader out of their comfort zone to consider where meaning and purpose can be found. While not directed at idolatry or other gross moral failings, in Ecclesiastes Qohelet makes a bold and prophetic call to action, imploring his hearers to cease searching for meaning in those places and pursuits where it cannot be grasped.

The way Qohelet used his office is usually inferred from the etymology of his name, with reference to 12:9: "Qohelet... taught knowledge to the people." Zimmerli very nearly takes a different route when discussing the similarities between the compilation in Ecclesiastes and Proverbs: "The epilogue 12:9 assertively establishes that Qohelet formed 'sayings', to which the headings in Proverbs 1:1; 10:1; 25:1 may be compared."[16] However, rather than discussing קהל with implications for Qohelet being an assembler of proverbs, he quickly makes the usual move to consider Qohelet with respect to the underlying verb קהל and the Greek title of the book. This is an approach followed by the vast majority of commentators. But considering the form of the book as discussed in this work, it might be worth reconsidering Qohelet as קהל not so much of the congregation, but of the sayings found in his book. In this respect, the relationship of 1:1a and 1:1b might be seen in the two parts of the book: the assembler of sayings, on the one hand, and the one examining life under the sun from the perspective of the son of David, on the other.

The Two Pairs of Bookends Together

The opening and closing frames together make clear that the contents within are not just worth reading, but, for those who are willing to have their values challenged, will bring them through appropriately chastised, but also corrected and redirected along the only path of any lasting value.

---

16. Zimmerli, "Prediger," 143, my translation.

Read together, the introduction and conclusion have a clear function in giving the necessary information to hear Qohelet properly. The opening introduces Qohelet, while the conclusion reminds the reader what they have just heard and from whom, and what they should do with these words.

Similarly, the opening poem gives the scope of Qohelet's study—the whole cosmos—while the concluding poem gives the scope of the subject—all those from youth to old age. These poetic bookends emphasize that vanity is indeed a global problem, affecting every person everywhere. For humans share the same earth, and will all die on that same earth. These two truths (the future of modern space travel notwithstanding) are truly the two great universals.

The primary contribution the epilogue makes is, as discussed above, with respect to the wisdom collections vis-à-vis the description of Qohelet as a collector of wisdom sayings. He collected and taught the people, and goaded them, through these sayings, to fear God and keep his commandments. As Ogden discusses the verb חקר (explore, 12:9), he says it "portrays the examining of life situations and the gathering together of like sayings";[17] this polyvalent understanding points to the alternating panels of the book, where life situations are indeed examined, and like sayings are indeed gathered together. 12:13 explains that the matter is now at an end (סוף דבר), as all that was discussed through these two modes of discourse has been heard (הכל נשמע).

The external bookends introduce and conclude the words of Qohelet, both his observations and experiences, as well as those sayings of others he has collated into this book. They describe the experience of reading, that it is a paradoxical and often frustrating experience—just as it was for Qohelet. Nonetheless, despite the frustrations, especially with regard to injustice and the folly of those who should know and behave better, the narrator re-emphasizes the orthodox truth (and Qohelet's dearly held hope) that God will one day execute his divine justice and right the wrongs experienced by Qohelet and his readers as vanity under the sun.

17. Ogden, *Qoheleth*, 209.

PART 4: THE BOOK'S BOOKENDS

When the external and internal bookends are considered, as well as the opening and closing poems, they reveal the body of the book: four pairs of alternating panels of observation and wisdom. The structure described throughout this book can be seen in outline overleaf.

SEEING WHAT QOHELET SAW

I   1:1-2 Introduction to Qohelet's Words

    1:1 Introduction to Qohelet

    1:2 The problem of vanity

II   1:3-11 Opening Poem

    1:3 The question: what gain?

    1:4-8 Five examples in the cosmos

    1:9-11 Response to the question

III   1:12-2:26 Observation Panel 1

    1:12-18 I saw the vanity of work

    2:1-11 I saw the vanity of achievement

    2:12-23 I saw the vanity of inheritance

    2:24-26 Conclusion: I saw two ways to work

IV   3:1-9 Wisdom Collection 1

    3:1 For everything a season

    3:2-8 "Sonnet" on time

    3:9 Is there any gain?

V   3:10—4:16 Observation Panel 2

    3:10-15 I saw beauty in the midst of burdens

    3:16-22 I saw justice in the context of death

    4:1-4 I saw that the problem of oppression makes death seem preferable

        4:5-6 Wisdom interlude: on work, rest and moderation

    4:7-16 I saw the solution to two vanities

VI   4:17—5:11 Wisdom Collection 2

    4:17—5:6 Honor God with your words and deeds

PART 4: THE BOOK'S BOOKENDS

5:7–8 Oppression is counter to natural (and God's) justice

5:9–11 If you see oppression, be assured that you can still sleep well

VII   **5:12—6:12 Observation Panel 3**

5:12–16 I saw an evil sickness

5:17–19 I saw God's good gift

6:1–12 I saw humanity

VIII   **7:1–14 Wisdom Collection 3**

7:1–6 What is better in the midst of death

7:7–12 What is better than the way of fools

7:13–14 Considering what God has made will teach us to live wisely

IX   **7:15—9:13 Observation Panel 4**

7:15–28a I've seen it all, and I did not find righteousness or wisdom

7:28b—8:9 I saw that God made people upright; they pursued many schemes

8:10–16 I saw the wicked confused with the righteous

8:17—9:10 I saw how hard it is for people to understand God

9:11–13 I saw there is wisdom in understanding the limits of human perception

X   **9:14—11:6 Wisdom Collection 4**

9:14—10:4 Might does not mean right

    10:5–7 Observation interlude: I saw foolish rulers

10:8–20 Negative examples of act-consequence

11:1–6 Limitations of human knowledge

XI 11:7—12:7 Concluding Poem

    11:7-10 Wisdom introduction on youth

    12:1 Remember your creator

    12:2-6 Five examples of death drawing near

    12:7 Remember your creator

XII 12:8-14 Conclusion to Qohelet's Words

    12:8-12 The problem of vanity and the importance of listening to wisdom

    12:13-14 Fear and obey God, the judge of everything

CONCLUSION

The first part of this book discussed the history of approaches to the structure of Ecclesiastes and sought to find a pathway which incorporated previous approaches but also forged a new direction. This meant identifying the keywords ראיתי/אראה, and, to a lesser extent other uses of ראה, as the way Qohelet's observations were highlighted. The book of Ecclesiastes was shown to be structured around alternating panels of Qohelet's first-person observations and then his collected wisdom.

The second part worked through Qohelet's observations in detail, demonstrating how the structure described in the first part worked in practice to give shape to the units within the panels.

The third part then looked at what was revealed either side of the observation panels, which were groupings of aphorisms, best described as wisdom collections or wisdom panels, which were distinguished negatively from the observation panels by their lack of ראיתי/אראה and lack of any first-person verbs or observation, and positively by their abundance of sayings or aphorisms which characterized these panels.

While the second and third parts concentrated on the alternating panels which form the body of the book, the fourth and concluding part discussed the bookends to the book, which included the opening and concluding poems (the internal bookends) and then the introduction and conclusion to Qohelet's words by the frame narrator (the external bookends). The poems presented the perspective of the book, while the introduction and conclusion to

Qohelet's words described what the readers could expect, namely the words of Qohelet in the midst of vanity (1:1–2) and Qohelet as the compiler of wisdom (12:9–10).

In conclusion, this book, from its very beginnings, was about trying to read Ecclesiastes better. What I have sought to demonstrate was that Ecclesiastes is best read as alternating panels of Qohelet's first-person observation and collected wisdom.

Having come across ראה, it is worth noting the exhortation from Proverbs 6:6, to "see (ראה) the ways [of the ant], so that you might become wise." This exhortation to gain wisdom by seeing reflects the description of the hypothetical wisdom school of Israel, with "an orientation that involves learning via critical observation and rational analysis," that "included close observation of both the natural world and human behavior."[1] This book has demonstrated that Qohelet's observations of his world and his collected wisdom typify not just the contents of the book, but importantly also, its structure.

Reading the book of Ecclesiastes according to the structure advanced within this book will not answer the questions of tone, dating, or authorship. Even though my own views on these may have occasionally been perspicuous as I have shown how the structure works in practice, it is describing the structure which has always been at the forefront. My hope is that the structure described in this book will enable a consensus to build around structure, which may for the first time provide a common foundation from which these other questions can continue to be investigated within the scholarly community, preached from in the church, and meditated upon by individuals.

---

1. Norman C. Habel, *Discerning Wisdom*, 13.

BIBLIOGRAPHY

Anderson, William H.U. "Ecclesiastes in the Intertextual Matrix of Ancient Near Eastern Literature." In *Reading Ecclesiastes Intertextually*, edited by Katherine Dell and Will Kynes, 157–75. Library of Hebrew Bible/Old Testament Studies. London: Bloomsbury T. & .T Clark, 2014.

Athas, George. *Ecclesiastes, Song of Songs*. Story of God Bible Commentary. Grand Rapids: Zondervan Academic, forthcoming (2020).

Bartholomew, Craig G. *Ecclesiastes*. Edited by Tremper Longman. Baker Commentary on the Old Testament Wisdom and Psalms. Accordance electronic. Grand Rapids: Baker Academic, 2009.

Bauckham, Richard J. *James*. New Testament Readings. New York: Routledge, 1999.

Beldman, David J. H. "Framed! Structure in Ecclesiastes." In *The Words of the Wise Are Like Goads: Engaging Qohelet in the 21st Century*, edited by Mark J. Boda, Tremper Longman, and Christian G. Rata, 137–61. Winona Lake, IN: Eisenbrauns, 2013.

Bickell, G. *Der Prediger über den Wert des Daseins*. Innsbruck: Wagner'sche Universitäts-Buchhandlung, 1884.

Braun, Rainer. *Kohelet und die Frühhellenistische Popularphilosophie*. Beihefte zur Zeitschrift für die alttestamentliche Wissenschaft 130. Berlin: de Gruyter, 1973.

Bullinger, E. W. *Figures of Speech Used in the Bible*. London: Eyre and Spottiswoode, 1898.

Castellino, Giorgio. "Qohelet and His Wisdom." *Catholic Biblical Quarterly* 30/1 (January 1968) 15–28.

Delitzsch, Franz. *Commentary on the Song of Songs and Ecclesiastes*. Translated by M. G. Easton. Clark's Foreign Theological Library 54. Edinburgh: T. & T. Clark, 1877.

Ellul, Jacques. *Reason for Being: A Meditation on Ecclesiastes*. Translated by Joyce M. Hanks. Grand Rapids: Eerdmans, 1990.

Fox, Michael V. *Ecclesiastes*. JPS Bible Commentary. Philadelphia: Jewish Publication Society, 2004.

———. "Frame-Narrative and Composition in the Book of Qohelet." *Hebrew Union College Annual* 48 (1977) 83-106.
———. *Qohelet and His Contradictions*. Journal for the Study of the Old Testament Supplement Series. Sheffield: Sheffield Academic, 1989.
———. *A Time to Tear Down and a Time to Build Up: A Rereading of Ecclesiastes*. Cambridge: Eerdmans, 1999.
Habel, Norman C. *Discerning Wisdom in God's Creation: Following the Way of Ancient Scientists*. Eugene, OR: Wipf & Stock, 2016.
Harvey, John D. *Listening to the Text: Oral Patterning in Paul's Letters*. ETS Studies Series. Grand Rapids: Baker, 1998.
Havelock, Eric Alfred. "The Alphabetization of Homer." In *Communicating Arts in the Ancient World*, edited by Eric Alfred Havelock and J. P. Herschbell, 3-21. New York: Hastings House, 1978.
Holmstedt, Robert D., John A. Cook, and Phillip S. Marshall. *Qoheleth: A Handbook on the Hebrew Text*. Baylor Handbook on the Hebrew Bible. Waco, Texas: Baylor University Press, 2017.
Jarick, John. "Ecclesiastes Among the Comedians." In *Reading Ecclesiastes Intertextually*, edited by Katherine Dell and Will Kynes, 176-88. Library of Hebrew Bible/Old Testament Studies. London: Bloomsbury T. & T. Clark, 2014.
Jerome. *St. Jerome: Commentary on Ecclesiastes*. Translated by Richard J. Goodrich and David J. D. Miller. Ancient Christian Writers. Mawhah, NJ: Paulist, 2012.
Jong, Stephan de. "A Book on Labour: The Structuring Principles and the Main Theme of the Book of Qohelet." *Journal for the Study of the Old Testament* 54 (1992) 107-16.
Koehler, Ludwig, and Walter Baumgartner, eds. *The Hebrew and Aramaic Lexicon of the Old Testament*. Leiden, Netherlands: Brill, 2000.
Krüger, Thomas. *Kohelet (Prediger)*. Biblischer Kommentar Altes Testament 14. Neukirchen-Vluyn: Neukirchener, 2000.
———, and O. C. Dean Jr. *Qoheleth: A Commentary*. Edited by Klaus Baltzer. Hermeneia. Accordance electronic. Minneapolis: Fortress, 2004.
Lee, Eunny P. *The Vitality of Enjoyment in Qohelet's Theological Rhetoric*. Beihefte zur Zeitschrift für die alttestamentliche Wissenschaft 353. Berlin: de Gruyter, 2005.
Loader, J. A. *Polar Structures in the Book of Qohelet*. New York: de Gruyter, 1979.
———. "Qohelet 3:2-8 – A 'Sonnet' in the Old Testament." *Zeitschrift für die alttestamentliche Wissenschaft* 81 (1969) 240-42.
Longman, Tremper. *The Book of Ecclesiastes*. New International Commentary on the Old Testament. Grand Rapids: Eerdmans, 1998.
Lowth, Robert. *Lectures on the Sacred Poetry of the Hebrews*. Translated by G. Gregory. 4th ed. London: Thomas Kegg, 1839.

BIBLIOGRAPHY

Luther, Martin. *Luther's Works*, vol. 15: *Ecclesiastes, Song of Solomon, and the Last Words of David*. Edited and translated by Jaroslav Pelikan. American ed. Saint Louis: Concordia, 1972.

Murphy, Roland E. *Ecclesiastes*. Word Biblical Commentary 23A. Waco, Texas: Accordance/Thomas Nelson, 1992.

Ogden, Graham S. *Qoheleth. Readings*. Sheffield: Sheffield Academic, 1987.

———, and Lynell Zogbo. *A Handbook on Ecclesiastes*. UBS Handbook Series. New York: United Bible Societies, 1997.

Peterson, David. *Commentary on Romans*. Biblical Theology for Christian Proclamation. Nashville: B&H, 2017.

Reinert, Andreas. *Die Salomofiktion: Studien zu Struktur und Komposition des Koheletbuches*. Wissenschaftliche Monographien zum Alten und Neuen Testament 126. Neukirchen-Vluyn: Neukirchener, 2010.

Salyer, Gary D. *Vain Rhetoric: Private Insight and Public Debate in Ecclesiastes*. Journal for the Study of the Old Testament Supplement Series. Sheffield: Sheffield Academic, 2001.

Seow, Choon-Leong. *Ecclesiastes*. Anchor Yale Bible. New Haven, CT: Yale University Press, 1997.

Shead, Andrew G. "Reading Ecclesiastes 'Epilogically.'" *Tyndale Bulletin* 48 (1997) 68–94.

Shields, Martin A. "Ecclesiastes and the End of Wisdom." *Tyndale Bulletin* 50 (1999) 118–42.

Siegfried, C. *Prediger und Hoheslied*. Handkommentar zum Alten Testament. 2/3/2. Göttingen: Vandenhoeck & Ruprecht, 1898.

Thaumaturgus, Gregory. "A Metaphrase of the Book of Ecclesiastes." Translated by S. D. F. Salmond. In *Fathers of the Third Century: Gregory Thaumaturgus, Dionysius the Great, Julius Africanus, Anatolius and Minor Writers, Methodius, Arnobius*, edited by Alexander Roberts, James Donaldson, and A. Cleveland Coxe. Ante-Nicene Fathers 6. New York: Christian Literature, 1885.

Waltke, Bruce K., and Michael P. O'Connor. *An Introduction to Biblical Hebrew Syntax*. Winona Lake, IN: Eisenbrauns, 1990.

Webb, Barry. *Five Festal Garments*. New Studies in Biblical Theology. Downers Grove, IL: InterVarsity, 2000.

Whitman, Cedric Hubbell. *Homer and the Heroic Tradition*. Cambridge, MA: Harvard University Press, 1967.

Whybray, Roger N. "The Identification and Use of Quotations in Ecclesiastes." In *Congress Volume: Vienna, 1980*, edited by J. A. Emerton, 455–61. Supplements to Vetus Testamentum 32. Leiden, Netherlands: Brill, 1981.

———. "Qoheleth, Preacher of Joy." *Journal for the Study of the Old Testament* 7/23 (July 1982) 87–98.

Wolters, Al. "Ecclesiastes and the Reformers." In *The Words of the Wise Are Like Goads: Engaging Qohelet in the 21st Century*, edited by Mark J. Boda, Tremper Longman, and Christian G. Rata, 55–68. Winona Lake, IN: Eisenbrauns, 2013.

BIBLIOGRAPHY

Wright, Addison G. "Additional Numerical Patterns in Qoheleth." *Catholic Biblical Quarterly* 45/1 (January 1983) 32–43.

———. "Riddle of the Sphinx: The Structure of the Book of Qoheleth." *Catholic Biblical Quarterly* 30/3 (July 1968) 313–34.

———. "The Riddle of the Sphinx Revisited: Numerical Patterns in the Book of Qoheleth." *Catholic Biblical Quarterly* 42/1 (January 1980) 38–51.

Zimmerli, Walther. "Das Buch Kohelet: Traktat oder Sentenzensammlung?" *Vetus Testamentum* 24/2 (April 1974) 221–30.

———. "Prediger." In *Sprüche-Prediger*, edited by Artur Weiser, 123–253. Das Alte Testament Deutsch. Göttingen: Vandenhoeck & Ruprecht, 1962.

www.ingramcontent.com/pod-product-compliance
Lightning Source LLC
Chambersburg PA
CBHW050834160426
43192CB00010B/2020